We Fed Them Cactus

WE FED THEM CACTUS

Fabiola Cabeza de Baca

With Drawings by Dorothy L. Peters

A Zia Book

UNIVERSITY OF NEW MEXICO PRESS

Albuquerque

TO LUIS

PREFACE

THIS IS THE STORY OF THE STRUGGLE of New Mexican Hispanos for existence on the Llano, the Staked Plains.

Through four generations, our family has made a living from this land—from cattle and sheep, and lately by selling curios, soda pop, gasoline and food to tourists traveling over U.S. Highway 66.

The stories of buffalo hunts and other events on the Llano were handed down to us by my grandfather's employees, by neighbors on the land, by our own ranch hands, and mostly by Papá, who spent a lifetime on the Ceja—the Cap Rock, and who traveled over the Llano before the fencing of the land.

In the description of the rodeo, I have used fictitious names, since it would be impossible for me to remember the names of all the people who were mentioned by El Cuate in his tales. It has been many years since he passed on. I was about ten years old when I heard him tell about the rodeos, the buffalo hunt, the mustangs, and other stories which I have tried to tell as nearly as El Cuate told them. Don Manuel Salcedo lived, but in real life he had another name.

All of the chapters present authentic historical facts. For dates which my informants did not have at the tip of the tongue, I consulted New Mexico histories and the Spanish archives of New Mexico. The dates of the founding of the chapels may not be exact, but they are within one or two years of the actual time. These dates I obtained from church records and from people who lived in different areas of the Llano.

On June 10, 1944, I visited Don Paco Baca in Puerto de Luna. He had reached his one-hundredth birthday on April second of that year. From him I secured the history of Puerto de Luna, Las Colonias, Santa Rosa and Antonchico. His health was failing but he had a clear memory—the dates which he gave me corroborated with those which I found in church records. He related many incidents about his trips over the Chihuahua and Santa Fe trails of commerce. Don Paco died on August 24, 1944.

For several years, I had tried to get a real picture of Spanish life on the Texas side of the Llano, and on July 26, 1948, I visited Doña Jesusita García de Chávez at the home of her sister-in-law, Doña Lola Otero de García. Both contributed to this history, and in telling it they relived their youth and early married years on the vast country of the Ceja and the Llano. From them I obtained names of places and people living on the bluffs of the Staked Plains from Texas into New Mexico.

It is fitting that I should dedicate this book to my brother, Luis María Cabeza de Baca IV. This is his book, for without his help, patience, and inspiration in assembling the material, I could not have compiled the Spanish American history of the Llano.

Luis has written a description of the buffalo hunt in his scrapbook:

"I knew many of the men who took part in the buffalo hunt. Among these were: Doroteo Vigil, Concepción Atencio, Santos López, Apolinar Almánzar, Teodoro Gonzáles, Benigno L. Benavídez, Longino Aragón, Luis Tapia, Eulogio Martínez, Juan José Quintana and others.

"My grandfather, the late Don Tomás D. Cabeza de Baca, used to employ a hunter and send, yearly, half a dozen wagons to the hunt. His two older sons, Manuel and Daniel, accompanied these hunting expeditions on two or three occasions in the 70's, merely for the sport. It was from them and others mentioned before that I acquired information for this article.

"I always delighted in listening to those men tell of the buffalo hunt, the fun which they had, the hardships endured—for all was not easy sailing. Blizzards overtook them and on the Llano a blizzard was terrible. There was no shelter and very little fuel available to use in building fires. Yucca roots (palmilla) and buffalo chips were the only materials that could be found suitable for fire building on the Llano proper.

"It was easy to get lost on the Llano, especially in a blinding snowstorm. Men were known to have become lost even on clear days, for on the Llano there were very few landmarks. Before it was settled, it was just an immense expanse of level land and sky.

"The route usually travelled by the *ciboleros* was the present site of Newkirk, the Laguna Colorada at the mouth of Bull Canyon past the south end of the Mesa Redonda and it climbed the Ceja where the present Norton is located. The gap where they climbed the Ceja was called, in those days, El Puerto de los Río-Abajeños."

THE *ricos* in New Mexico, as mentioned in this story, were those who owned land. Many of the Spanish families were given grants of land comprising from several thousand to a million acres each. These families had large herds of sheep and cattle. There were also merchants in the larger towns who owned wagon trains that went into Chihuahua and, later, into the States. These merchants amassed fortunes and they, too, were in the *rico* class.

Many historians and writers have contended that there was no wealth in colonial New Mexico, but there was. It was strictly a feudal system and the wealth was in the hands of the few. The *ricos* of colonial days lived in splendor with many servants and slaves. Their haciendas were similar to the Southern plantations. To those coming from what was then the United States of America, the life of the New Mexican *ricos* was not understood because they kept their private lives secure from outsiders. The latter judged all New Mexicans by the people of the streets, since the families of the wealthy were never seen outside the home and the church. There were family gatherings, but as the families of influence married among themselves, there was not much opportunity for outsiders to learn their ways of living.

There are different ways of reckoning wealth and a set pattern does not exist and may never be found. People who live from the soil have abundant living and, compared with that of the wage earner, it can be classed as wealth. On the Llano, in the days of open range, there were men who ran thousands of head of cattle and sheep. The Baca brothers from Upper Las Vegas—Don José, Don Simón, Don Aniceto and Don Pablo—jointly were running half a million head of sheep in the 1870's.

Fabiola Cabeza de Baca

Santa Fe
June 1, 1950

CONTENTS

I. THE LLANO

1. Loneliness without Despair

THE LLANO IS A GREAT PLATEAU. Its sixty thousand square miles tip almost imperceptibly from fifty-five hundred feet above sea level in northwest New Mexico, to two thousand feet in northwest Texas.

From the Canadian River, the Llano runs southward some four hundred miles. The Pecos River and the historic New Mexican town of Las Vegas mark its ragged western edge, while two hundred miles to the east lie Palo Duro Canyon—once the goal of Spanish buffalo hunters—and the city of Amarillo, steeped in the traditions of Texas cattle-raising.

Between these boundaries are the settlements, whistlestops, trading posts, chapels, ranch headquarters and homesteader's houses—some new, some old, many abandoned—which tell the story of more than a hundred years of living on the Llano.

Curving along the Llano's high northern and western rim is the Cap Rock, the rough-hewn Ceja, or eyebrow, above the plain.

No other land, perhaps, is more varied in its topography than the Ceja and the Llano country. As one descends Cañon del Agua Hill from Las Vegas, a full view of this great stretch of country greets the sight. There are myriads of hills, peaks, wooded mesas, canyons and valleys. The Montoso, wooded land, extends for miles and miles. In the distance one can see Conchas Mesa, Corazón and Cuervo peaks, the Variadero Tableland, and many other hillocks. Traveling on, descending hills, crossing arroyos, one reaches Cabra Spring. This is an oasis, a spring of sweet water which saved many a traveler from dying of thirst on his way to the buffalo and Comanche country. Later it was a watering place for an overnight stop on the way to the sheep and cattle territory.

It is unbelievable that in a country where rain is scant, there can be so many springs gushing from the earth in the most secluded places. There are lakes all along the land, some made by rains, some fed by springs from the hills. If rains are plentiful, these lakes may be filled the year round; if rains are few, the lakes may dry up from evaporation.

There are deep canyons in the hills, seemingly inaccessible, yet the old-timers knew every canyon, spring and lake from Las Vegas to the Panhandle of Texas.

After passing Cabra Spring, one comes in view of the Luciano and Palomas mesas, Tucumcari Peak, Cuervo Hill and, in the distance, Pintada Mesa. Bull Canyon of the Luciano Mesa presents one of the picturesque panoramas of the area. Its red coloring, from red earth and rocks surrounding it, is typical of the land and a sight comparable, perhaps, to the Grand Canyon of Arizona.

From Cañon del Agua Hill to Luciano Mesa, the vegetation includes juniper, piñon, yucca, mesquite, sagebrush, gramma and buffalo grasses, as well as lemita, prickly pear, and pitahaya. There are wild flowers in abundance, and when the spring comes rainy, the earth abounds in all colors imaginable. The fields of oregano and cactus, when in full bloom, can compete with the loveliest of gardens.

2

It is a lonely land because of its immensity, but it lacks nothing for those who enjoy Nature in her full grandeur. The colors of the skies, of the hills, the rocks, the birds and the flowers, are soothing to the most troubled heart. It is loneliness without despair. The whole world seems to be there, full of promise and gladness.

Leaving the Luciano and Palomas, the Ceja country, and traveling east and south, one comes upon the great Llano, so extensive that one must see it to realize its vastness. For miles and miles, as far as the eye can see, is the expanse of level land. Here are mesquite, prickly pear, yucca, and grass, grass, grass.

THERE is little similarity between the Llano of today and that of the last century. The Llano, then, was an endless territory of grass and desert plants, with nothing to break the monotony except the horizon and the sky. In the days of the buffalo and the Coman-

3

che, the Llano was uninhabited and dangerous. The buffalo hunters knew the waterholes and springs, yet they had to be careful to follow the right trails; otherwise they would perish.

The early Spanish colonists had settled along the rivers in north central New Mexico, using the surrounding land for pasturing their sheep and cattle. They did not extend their grazing because of the aridity of the country south and west of the Rio Grande, and because northern pastures along the smaller rivers lie in the cold belt where rigorous winters make it more difficult for stock to survive. The frequent raids of the Navajos were another deterrent to increasing the herds.

While the colonists had received all protection available against warring Indian tribes during Spanish rule, when Mexico gained its independence from Spain in 1821, the New Mexicans were left to survive by their own resourcefulness. They found it prohibitive to augment their livestock. Indians came down on the settlements, killing herders and driving off sheep, cattle and horses. Between 1821 and 1840, flocks and herds had to be reduced to numbers small enough to be tended close to the settlements. At night all livestock had to be corralled in the *placitas,* the squares within the walls of houses.

THE New Mexican home of the *rico,* or landowner, as I heard my grandmother describe it, was a fortress in itself. It was built around a square, with living quarters on one side. Another side comprised storerooms, granaries and workshops. On the third side was constructed the *cochera* for the family coach, *carretas,* and wagons. The fourth end, which completed the square, was a high wall with one entrance—a massive gate of hand-hewn timbers. Through this gate, the horses, mules, cattle, sheep, goats, and pigs were driven at night. The outer walls of the flat-roofed

4

adobe houses were built high and pierced with *troneras,* loopholes for fighting Indians.

Livestock had to be kept close to the settlements and under close surveillance of the herders. Consequently, the range near the towns and villages became denuded of the natural browse, which for years had pastured the stock. Traditionally, meat had been the main fare on New Mexican tables, but with the decrease in livestock, the supply became more and more scarce.

THE Llano and Ceja country were well known to the New Mexicans who ventured forth as Indian fighters and to hunt the buffalo. They brought back tales of the good pastures and the extensive territory beyond the mountains.

The sheep and cattle owners traveled eastward, and on the Ceja and the Llano found the Promised Land. There, where the mountains end and the plains begin, they found grama and buffalo grass growing as tall as the cattle.

The best pastures were on the Ceja, the Cap Rock area at the top of the Staked Plains. As one descends south and east from Las Vegas, all the country is known as the Llano, and it is the history of this section, of its people and their lives, which this book tells. To one living on the American plains of the Middle West, so level and flat, the land on the bluffs of the Staked Plains, with its rocky hills, juniper, mesquite, and piñon, may not seem a llano, but to New Mexicans, because of the drop of two or three thousand feet from the peaks, it is not the Sierras, and they have called it the Llano—the wide open spaces.

IN 1840, the sheep owners started sending herders with their flocks into the Ceja and the Llano, and the Hispanos continued to prosper in the sheep industry for more than half a century.

In those days a man had to be courageous to face the many dangers confronting lonely living far from the populated areas, yet there seems to have been no lack of men who were willing to follow the herds for the employers, the *patrones*. In feudal times, there were many poor people who became indebted to the *ricos,* and the rich were never at a loss to find men to be sent with flocks of sheep. Then, of course, herding was one of the few kinds of employment available in New Mexico. If a man became indebted to a *rico,* he was in bond slavery to repay. Those in debt had a deep feeling of honesty, and they did not bother to question whether the system was right or wrong. Entire families often served a *patrón* for generations to meet their obligations.

If the flock of the *patrón* ran into thousands, he employed a *mayordomo,* or manager, and several overseers, called *caporales.* The *caporal* was in charge of the herders, and had to see that the sheep were provided proper quarters in the different seasons. He furnished the sheep camps with provisions, and it was his duty to make sure that water was available for the *partidas* under the care of each herder. A *partida* usually consisted of a thousand head of sheep. The *caporales* worked under the *mayordomo,* or directly under the *patrón* if no manager were employed.

I can remember my paternal grandfather's sheep camps and the men who worked for him. They were loyal people, and as close to us as our own family. They were, every one of them, grandfather's *compadres,* for he and grandmother had stood as sponsors in baptism or marriage to many of their children.

Lambing season was a trying one, since the range was extensive. This happened in the early spring, and the weather on the Llano can be as changeable as the colors of the rainbow. If the season was rainy, it went hard with the sheep and many lambs were lost. If there had been a dry spell the year before, the ewes

6

came out poorly and it was difficult for the mothers bringing in young lambs. Sheep raising was always a gamble until the day when feed became plentiful with the change in transportation facilities.

In order to save ewes and lambs during a cold spell, the herders built fires around the herds. The fires were kept burning day and night until better weather came to the rescue. Quite often the *patrones* and their sons, who might have just come back from Eastern colleges, helped during lambing.

Shearing the sheep was done in the summer and there were professional shearers who went from camp to camp each year. This was a bright spot in the life of the herders, for then they had a touch of the outside world. Among the shearers and herders there were always musicians and poets, and I heard Papá tell of pleasant evenings spent singing and storytelling, and of *corridos* composed to relate events which had taken place. These poets and singers were like the troubadours of old. The *corridos* dealt with the life of the people in the communities and ranches; they told of unrequited love, of death, of tragedies and events such as one reads about in the newspapers today.

The sheepherder watched his flock by day, traveling many miles while the sheep grazed on the range. As his flock pastured, he sat on a rock or on his coat; he whittled some object or composed songs or poetry until it was time to move the flock to water or better pasture. Many of the *corridos* are an inheritance from the unlettered sheepherder. At night he moved his flock to camp, a solitary tent where he prepared his food and where he slept. If there were several camps close to each other, the herders gathered at one tent for companionship.

In winter the sheepherder's life was dreary. Coming into his old tent at night, he had to prepare for possible storms. The wood for his fire might be wet, and with scarcely any matches, perhaps only a flint stone to light it, his hands would be numb before he had any warmth. He might not even have wood, for in many parts of the Llano there is no wood, and cowchips had to serve as fuel.

He went to sleep early to the sound of the coyote's plaintive cry, wondering how many lambs the wolves or coyotes might carry away during the night. The early call of the turtle dove and the bleating of lambs were his daily alarm clock, and he arose to face another day of snow, rain, or wind. Yet he always took care of his sheep, and I have never known any mishap due to the carelessness of the herder. The *caporales* traveled on horseback from camp to camp in all kinds of weather to make sure that all was well with the herders and the flocks.

I knew an old man who worked for my maternal grandmother for many years. Often I accompanied my grandmother to the sheep camp on the Salado, and I always came back with a feeling of loneliness. Yet, at camp, the old man always seemed happy. If he was not at camp when we arrived, we found him by listening for his whistling or singing in the distance. When I think about the herders on the endless Llano, I know that they are the unsung heroes of an industry which was our livelihood for generations.

II. EL CUATE

2. The Night It Rained

WE HAD JUST FINISHED BRANDING at the Spear Bar Ranch. For a whole week we had been rounding up cattle and branding each bunch as they were brought in from the different pastures.

As we sat out on the patio of our ranch home, I watched Papá leaning back in his chair against the wall of the house. He always did that when he was happy. The coolness of the evening brought relief from the heat and dust in the noisy corrals during the day.

The hard dirt floor of the patio always had a certain coolness about it. Just a few nights before, the boys had been in the mood to renovate it. They brought a load of dirt, which we sprinkled with water and spread over with burlap sacks. We had such fun tramping it down. We made it a game by jumping on it until the soil was packed hard. This was repeated until we had a solid, even patio floor. Around it the boys built a supporting wall of rock filled in with mud.

Our home was a rambling structure without plan. It was built of the red rock from the hills around us, put together with mud. The walls were two feet thick. Viewed from front, the house had an L shape, but from the back, it appeared as a continuous sequence of rooms.

We had pine floors in the front room and dining room and

9

the other rooms had hard-packed dirt floors. The *despensa* occupied a space of twelve hundred square feet. This room served as a storeroom, summer kitchen, and sleeping quarters when stray cowboys dropped in on a snowy or rainy night. The windows had wooden bars and so had the door.

The *cochera* adjacent to the *despensa* was a relic of the days of carriages and horses. When automobiles came into use, it became a garage, but we always called it the *cochera*. The front had two large doors which opened wide for the carriage to be brought out, and the hole for the carriage tongue always remained on the doors to remind us of horse and buggy days.

The roof on our house was also of hard-packed mud. Many years later, it boasted a tin roof. The dirt roof had been supported by thick rectangular *vigas,* or beams, which remained even after we had the tin roof.

All the rooms were spacious and our home had a feeling of hospitality. We had only the most necessary pieces of furniture. We had Papá's big desk in the front room and dozens of chairs with wide arms. Over the mantel of the corner fireplace, in the dining room, hung a large antique mirror. Grandmother's wedding trunk, brought over the Chihuahua Trail, stood against a wall. It was made of leather, trimmed with solid brass studs. We had no clothes closets, but there were plenty of trunks in every room. Mamá's wedding trunk, made of brass, tin and wood, was the shape of a coffer. Papá's trunk was very similar. We all had trunks.

The most necessary pieces of furniture were the beds. Of these, we had plenty, but many a night three of us slept in one bed, and if we were inconvenienced we were recompensed. Our sudden guests came from different *ranchos,* and they always had wonderful tales and news to relate.

Tonight we had no guests. We were a happy family enjoying the evening breeze with hopes for rain. The cowboys did not need chairs; they were stretched out on the ground with their hands clasped behind their heads as a protection from the hard dirt floor of the patio—a typical relaxation from the day's labors.

I can never remember when Papá was not humming a tune, unless his pipe was in his mouth. Tonight he was just looking up at the sky. As the clouds began to gather towards the east, he said, "We may have some rain before morning. Those are promising clouds. If rain does not come before the end of the month, we will not have grass for winter grazing. Our pastures are about burnt up."

From the time I was three years old—when I went out to the Llano for the first time—I began to understand that without rain our subsistence would be endangered. I never went to bed without praying for rain. I have never been inclined to ask for favors from heaven, but for rain, I always pleaded with every saint and the Blessed Mother. My friends in the city would be upset when rain spoiled a day's outing, but I always was glad to see it come. In the years of drought, Papá's blue eyes were sad, but when the rains poured down, his eyes danced like the stars in the heavens on a cloudless night. All of us were happy then. We could ask for the moon and he would bring it down.

Good years meant fat cattle and no losses, and that, we knew would bring more money. We had never been poor, because those who live from the land are never really poor, but at times Papá's cash on hand must have been pretty low.

If that ever happened, we did not know it. Money in our lives was not important; rain was important. We never counted our money; we counted the weeks and months between rains. I could always tell anyone exactly to the day and hour since the last rain,

11

and I knew how many snowfalls we had in winter and how many rains in spring. We would remember an unusually wet year for a lifetime; we enjoyed recalling it during dry spells.

Rain for us made history. It brought to our minds days of plenty, of happiness and security, and in recalling past events, if they fell on rainy years, we never failed to stress that fact. The droughts were as impressed on our souls as the rains. When we spoke of the Armistice of World War I, we always said, "The drought of 1918 when the Armistice was signed."

We knew that the east wind brought rain, but if the winds persisted from other directions we knew we were doomed. The northwest wind brought summer showers.

From childhood, we were brought up to watch for signs of rain. In the New Year, we started studying the *Cabañuelas*. Each day of January, beginning with the first day, corresponded to each month of the year. Thus, the first of January indicated what kind of weather we would have during the first month. The second day told us the weather for February and the third for March. When we reached the thirteenth of January, we started again. This day would tell us the weather for December. After twenty-four days, we knew for sure whether the *Cabañuelas* would work for us or not. If the days representing the months backward and forward coincided, we could safely tell anyone whether to expect rain in April or in May. The *Cabañuelas* are an inheritance from our Spanish ancestors and are still observed in Spain and Latin America.

From the Indians we learned to observe the number of snowfalls of the season. If the first snow fell on the tenth of any month, there would be ten falls that year. If it fell on the twentieth, we would be more fortunate: there would be twenty snowfalls during the cold months.

12

We faithfully watched the moon for rain. During the rainy season, the moon had control of the time the rains would fall. April is the rainy month on the Llano, and if no rain fell by the end of April, those versed in astrology would tell us that we could still expect rain in May if the April moon was delayed. There were years when the moons came behind schedule.

Whether these signs worked or not, we believed in them thoroughly. To us, looking for rain, they meant hope, faith, and a trust in the Great Power that takes care of humanity.

Science has made great strides. Inventions are myriad. But no one has yet invented or discovered a method to bring rain when wanted or needed. As a child, prayer was the only solution

to the magic of rain. As I grew older and I began to read of the discoveries of science, I knew that someday the Llano would have rain at its bidding. On reaching middle age, I am still praying for rain.

My mind still holds memories of torrential rains. Papá would walk from room to room in the house watching the rain from every window and open door. I would follow like a shadow. My heart would flutter with joy to see Papá so radiant with happiness.

Often before the rain was over, we would be out on the patio. I would exclaim, "We are getting wet, Papá!" "No, no," he would say. He wanted to feel the rain, to know that it was really there. How important it was in our lives!

After the rain subsided, off came my shoes and I was out enjoying the wetness, the rivulets. The arroyo flood would be coming down like a mad roaring bull. Papá and I would stand entranced watching the angry red waters come down. The arroyo, usually dry and harmless, would come into its own defying all living things, enjoying a few hours of triumph. A normally dry arroyo is treacherous when it rains.

If the rain came at night, we were cheated of the pleasure of enjoying the sight. Yet there was a feeling of restfulness as we listened to the rain on the roof. The raindrops on the windows showed like pearls, and to us they were more valuable than the precious stones themselves.

A few rains and then sun, and the grass would be as tall as the bellies of the cows grazing upon it. And Papá was happy.

A storm on the Llano is beautiful. The lightning comes down like arrows of fire and buries itself on the ground. At the pealing of thunder, the bellowing of cattle fills the heart of the listeners with music. A feeling of gladness comes over one as the heavens open in downpour to bathe Mother Earth. Only those ever watching and waiting for rain can feel the rapture it brings.

Papá never saw the lightning. He was too busy watching for the raindrops.

On the Llano, although rains come seldom, the cowboy is always prepared with his yellow slicker tied on the back of the saddle, always hopeful and waiting for rain. The straps on the back of a saddle were put there to hold the rider's raincoat.

As we sat on the patio that evening, the wind suddenly changed and the odor of rain reached our nostrils.

El Cuate, the Twin, who was the ranch cook, spat out a wad of tobacco as he said, "I knew it would rain before the end of the month. The moon had all signs of rain when it started. The signs never fail."

We were always glad when El Cuate spat out his tobacco. We knew he was in the mood for storytelling. What stories he could tell! There were stories of buffalo hunts, Indian attacks, about Comanche trade, of rodeos and fiestas.

El Cuate was an old man, and he had a history behind him. He was a real western character reared on the Llano. To me, he seemed to have sprung from the earth. He was so much a part of the land of the Llanos that he might have just grown from the soil as the grass and the rocks and the hills.

Looks, he had none. He was short in stature, blind in one eye, with an aquiline nose and sensuous mouth guarded by a long tapering red mustache. His skin was tanned by the sun of the prairies and the wrinkles on it portrayed the endurance and hardships of his life. His hair was gray with signs of sandiness in it. His hands were rough and wrinkled, showing that his life had not been idle. He used his hands for talking as well as for working, so they were always in evidence; they were interesting hands.

15

My brother, Luis, rose from the ground and started to leave saying, "I am going to hit the hay. Today has been a day. I am too tired even to listen to you tonight, Cuate."

El Cuate laughingly answered, "You young fellows are soft, you can't take it. Take your Papá there, although he is still a young man, he and I have seen some tough times. Branding today is play. You should have been part of the rodeos I experienced."

I could never let an opportunity pass of hearing his adventures when he showed signs of talking.

Before he had time to take another chew of tobacco, I said, "Please tell us about life on the Llano, Cuate."

"*Pues,* señores," he started. This was the introductory phrase which always turned into a tale by El Cuate.

We knew we must make ourselves comfortable, for it might be months or years before he would be in a storytelling mood. Even Luis forgot he was tired and resumed his resting position.

Papá was a man of few words. The only time he became talkative was after a rain and then he would compete with El Cuate.

Tonight Papá was happy. The clouds were gathering in the east. This was a sure sign of rain before morning, so he made himself comfortable by leaning his chair against the wall. I knew then that he meant to stay up with us until the first raindrops came. Listening to El Cuate would help pass away the time.

I watched El Cuate take a chew of tobacco as I heard Papá start him off. "I believe it was in this spot or just where the east windmill stands that I was initiated into my first rodeo. I was fifteen years old and fresh from school."

"Yes, sir," replied El Cuate, reminiscing. "I remember that rodeo," and as if prompted, began a tale of a lifetime.

16

3. The Rodeo

"IT WAS HERE ON THE CARRIZITO that we held the rodeo that year," El Cuate began. "It was in 1886 and we had had an unusually dry spring. We held the rodeo in July."

"Don Manuel Salcedo, (may he rest in peace), was the promoter of the rodeo. He was an aristocrat if there ever was one, and he was wealthy. His herds roamed from the Salado to the Llano Estacado, although by 1886 he was being pushed back by the XIT Syndicate which had moved in the year before.

"There were two rodeos during the year. One was held in early summer and the other just before the fall, unless it was a dry year, and then there would be only one. A rodeo, in those days truly meant a roundup, not a public exhibition.

"Señor Antonio Almanzar was the cook and I was his assistant, with Santiago Estrada as the chore boy. Señor Antonio, who was as stern as he was jovial, was Don Manuel's handyman and a better man he could not have picked; honesty and loyalty towards his *patrón* were his best qualities.

"I can still hear his voice. Before daybreak, we awakened to his cry:

" 'Juan, Santiago, Felipe, it is almost daylight, and you lie

17

there as if you were gentlemen of leisure! You have no consciences to warn you that you are stealing precious time from your *patrón*. Get up, and to your duties. Juan, get the *remuda*. Santiago, start the fire for the coffee. Felipe, roll up the beds and get the saddles ready.'

"After sleeping on the hard ground, you would think that we were glad to get up, but we liked our sleep as well as you youngsters do," he said to me and Luis, winking with his white eye and looking at Papá. Papá was not an early riser but his children and the cowboys were up at dawn.

El Cuate, smiling, continued, "Santiago was bold and he answered Señor Antonio, 'If you were not so conscientious, Don Manuel would not be swimming in wealth while we drink black bitter coffee and eat black bread.'

"Felipe just turned over and growled, but when Señor Antonio's voice sounded like thunder, weakly one by one, we got up and started the morning chores, rubbing our eyes as if that would help us see in the dark.

"Juan had been gone almost an hour for the *remuda,* the string of horses.

"We had few matches in those days, but we carried candles which we lighted by striking two flint stones with a piece of cured cloth between them. Santiago lighted a small candle beside his bed, put on his boots and he was dressed. He then lighted the sticks which Señor Antonio had been gathering all the while, and soon a big bonfire was crackling and lighting the surrounding sleepers, who like white specters were seen rising from their beds as if to the sound of an alarm clock.

"The morning was as still as death, with only the hobbling of the horses heard in the distance or an occasional howl of a coyote which to the human ear sounded like a whole pack. The sound

18

of the coffee mill furnished the music to the late risers, and not until the smell of the boiling coffee from the black can on the coals reached their nostrils, did they jump up from their happy dreams to a long day—rounding up cattle for the annual rodeo.

"Before all the men were around the breakfast circle, Juan's whistling was heard as he was approaching with the horses. *Yip! Yip!* went out from the cowboys, meaning 'Good morning and thanks for letting us sleep that extra hour.' Our breakfast was of beans, prunes, sourdough bread, jerky or fresh meat, and black coffee.

"Every cattleman who owned a thousand head of cattle or more made up a rodeo with his hired hands and as many stray men as wanted to go along. A stray man was usually the hired hand of a small cattle owner, or he might be the owner himself.

"Every rodeo had a *mayordomo,* and for this one we had Don Andrés Garduño, Don Manuel Salcedo's head man. We all respected Don Andrés, a sturdy upright fellow, who knew how to give orders. When he gave them I always thought he should have been a general. I feared him more than I did Colonel Canby at Valverde during the Civil War."

El Cuate brushed away a tear as he continued:

"There were many fearless men in those days. They had to be or they would not have followed the rodeos.

"Don Andrés always mounted his horse when he gave orders, and as he started to give the command that day, he half leaned on the saddle:

" 'Manuel García and Teles Urbán, follow the trail to Paloma; Andrés Guzmán and Juan Arellano, round up the cattle on the Laguna Colorada; Felipe Tafoya and Carmen Sierra, follow the old trail into San Lorenzo; Felipe Mora and Juan Peralta, your journey will be towards the Mesa Rica; Narciso Paez, Jua-

19

nito Trujillo, and Rafael Baca, scour the Monte de Pajarito for cattle; Fidel Tapia and Mauricio Lucero, will go to Don Tomás Cabeza de Baca's sheep camp and tell Señor Ramón, the *caporal,* to send me five fat lambs. Ride until you find the sheep, for we must feed our men well or their *patrones* will take me for a miser.'

"As the men on horseback took to different directions, Señor Antonio and I watched them until the last man disappeared over the horizon. It was our job to feed the men, so back we went to our camp. Santiago had been cleaning beans by the campfire and we were always glad to see daylight for that meant fewer pebbles in our beans. As he cleaned the beans, he kept up a weird monotonous song until Señor Antonio, out of patience, called to him in rather strong language, 'Santiago, change your tune or I shall be singing it myself.'

"Santiago was a good worker, but he was born to try men's patience. He seldom changed expression, so we never knew when he was serious or when he was trying to mortify us. He changed the tune of his song but he started another one so mournful that he drove me to desperation. To pass away the time, the cowboys would come to terms only by selling what annoyed their companions. I had to do something to stop Santiago's mournful tune, so I said, 'Sell me your tune and remember after it is paid for, it belongs to me and you cannot use it without my permission.' Santiago thought for a moment, then he replied, 'I'll sell it to you for that new quirt that you brought from Revuelto.'

"The quirt was a priceless possession, but I had to respond to the challenge so I said, 'The quirt is yours and the tune is mine.' While we waited for the return of the *vaqueros,* the cowboys, with the herds, we had to keep up our spirits with jokes and songs or tales.

"At the first sound of the *Yip! Yip!* I put wood into the fire to start the coffee boiling in the same black can which I had used at so many rodeos.

"It was toward midafternoon before all the men returned to camp with hundreds of cattle to be branded. The quiet air of the camp was soon broken by the bawling of cattle and the country became a Sodom of noise and dust from all directions with the *vaqueros* yelling and the cattle tramping.

"The men who remained at camp had eaten their noon meal. They saddled their horses and started out to meet the approaching herds in order to relieve these *vaqueros* who were bringing in the cattle.

"I can still see each man as he galloped into camp, sweaty and dusty. Santiago, our mascot, had the chore of unsaddling sweaty horses as the men dismounted. We watered the horses and then he turned them over to the *caballerango* in charge of them.

"The men were always hungry and I felt great pride because they praised my cooking.

"While the men were eating, the branding irons were being heated to start the marking of cattle.

"Herd after herd approached the camp, until we had about a thousand head of cattle. I saw rodeos where two and three thousand head were gathered for one day's branding. Sí señores, there was almost one cow to each blade of grass in those days." (This, of course, entitled El Cuate to a fresh chew of tobacco.)

"When all was ready, Don Andrés mounted his cutting horse and, with four of his best hands, started separating the cattle with Don Manuel's brand."

"The cutting horse was swift and had plenty of sense, and when its rider spied a cow with his brand, the horse knew which cow or steer he had to follow, and he would plunge after the ani-

mal, driving it out of its herd and into the day herd with a quick rush. The cattle which had to be branded were separated, as I said, and this bunch was called the day herd.

"We had no corrals in those days, but the men on horseback made the enclosure which held the cattle together and, believe me, those longhorns were vicious-looking animals. But since they were used to being rounded up, they were no trouble, unless there were stampedes.

"I remember rodeos when it took days and days to round up the cattle. But by 1886, rodeos had taken smaller proportions as there was less territory to cover. In my youth, the rodeo boundaries were the sierras to the north, the Texas line to the east, what is now Roswell on the south and the Manzano mountains on the west.

"On that first day of the Carrizito rodeo, we only branded one hundred head of heifers and steers with Don Manuel's brand.

"The cowboys all were expert riders and ropers, but we had professionals. Teles Urbán and Carmen Sierra never missed an animal from the first throw of the lasso, and in every rodeo in which they took part they were the roping hands.

"The branding was no different from what you did today, only it seems to me that the men were more hardened and fearless than you boys.

"It seems only yesterday that we were branding, and that I saw Carmen Sierra ride through the herd, throw the rope over the calves' heads or hind feet and drag them toward the branding irons where the ground crew waited. There was Tito Lucero, ready to grab the calf and he threw the animal down. In the wink of an eye, Laureano García had taken hold of it by the front, grabbed the foreleg, and pinned the neck down with his knee while Juan Arellano (in a sitting posture) pulled the hind leg towards him—and the animal was ready for the brand and other operations. The boys on the ground crew knew whose calf it was, and the roper always announced whose brand the calf's mother bore, so there were no mistakes.

"There were professional branders like your Papá is today. He always followed the branding iron—but that's education for you, for those who could not read might have put the letters upside down.

"The burning hot iron was put on the proper place and the brand imprinted. Another man did the earmarking and another the castrating. The only difference from today is that in order to get through with the many herds, more men did the different chores which a small crew performs now.

"Cattle with various brands roamed all over the unfenced Llano, and the cowboys from each outfit were constantly on the watch for their stock as they rode the range all through the year. The spaciousness of the land did not permit them to know

23

exactly how many head of each brand grazed on the plains, but the rodeos brought many surprises.

"The evening meal was the social affair of the day. Señor Antonio and I were very popular with the boys—they called us mamá, sweetheart, or honey. We fed not only the rodeo outfit, but many of the cattle owners who dropped in for meals if the rodeo grounds were within riding distance to their ranches.

"Besides the lambs which we got from nearby camps, we also butchered one or two mavericks, calves which had escaped the branding iron the previous year and belonged to the first cowboy who caught them and put his brand on them. Señor Antonio and I always picked the fattest ones to feed our men and it took a lot for a bunch of cowboys. Their work was hard and the hours were long between meals.

"After supper the boys not on night duty would gather around the campfires and sing ballads and *corridos*. Juan Arellano was a good singer, but there were many others, and we had poets, too. Our poet and storyteller on that rodeo was Fidel Tapia, and he certainly had imagination and good memory. His father and I had been *Comancheros*—Indian "traders"—and buffalo hunters together. As the darkness fell upon us, the music from the different groups around the campfire came softly, bringing cheer to the men tired from the day's labors.

"The first night, the men retired early and before the last embers died the boys were resting on their hard beds on the ground. Each man used his saddle for a pillow, wrapped himself with a blanket and took chances on lying on safe soil for the night.

"The bellowing of cattle, the bawling of calves, the sounds of hoofs stirring up dust, and the hobbling of horses were the nightly lullabies which brought sound sleep to us, for we were accustomed to it.

"The herds had to be guarded at night because it had taken almost the whole day to round up the cattle and all of them had not been separated.

"There were four shifts, with two or three men to the shift. Each shift was called a *cuarto*. The first shift was the coveted one and it usually went to the foreman's favorites, but the cowboys were good sports and, although they grumbled, they took it like men. Yet in the old days before 1886, there were even killings on account of the shifts. Nowadays the men, like the cattle, have become more tame. I felt sorry for the boys, for they had chosen a hard vocation and it was their cross to bear.

"The cattle bedded down at night and the night riders rode around and around the herd whistling or singing. The music kept the cattle aware of the riders and prevented stampedes.

"I MUST tell you about the stampedes. They were terrible. They could be started by a sudden peal of thunder, a large dry weed blown towards the herd, a coyote's yelp, or often a cause unknown.

"The cattle would dash together, as if driven, and run as fast as their hoofs could carry them. Woe to the man caught in their path! If his horse stumbled or if he were thrown from his seat, it was sure death.

"The stampede which remains vivid in my memory happened in 1880, just as we reached Plaza Larga with the rodeo.

"By the time we had finished supper and the first shift started, the sky had clouded and we knew the storm would reach our camp before morning. Flashes of lightning were visible even while we were eating. We knew we were in for a good soaking, but what worried the boys was the possibility of a stampede.

"There would be no sleep that night and all the boys had to be on hand if needed.

"The clouds moved faster and faster, and with them came flashes of lightning and heavy thunder. The lightning which struck in every direction made the cattle restless and the boys were on the alert.

"The storm reached its peak and down came the rain in heavy sheets. The whole camp was in confusion and all at once lightning struck close to the herd. The stampede started. The boys tried to head it off, but the wind was against them. They had to be careful that they would not be knocked down. The lightning flashes made everything visible, but just as quickly the darkness seemed more intense.

"The boys kept whistling and singing but the cattle paid no heed. They were on the run. The boys were all trying to hold them down at the risk of their lives; they whistled; they rode hard—but the cattle were beyond control.

"Señor Antonio and I had stayed in the wagon and all we could do was pray, for hardened as we were, we remembered God and we prayed. We knew there might not be one of the men left if the cattle struck their paths. In a stampede the cattle stay together; they become blinded as they run. And the cattle that night were not only blind, they were mad.

"I do not know how many miles the cattle had traveled, but at dawn, one by one the boys came back to camp exhausted. The rain had stopped and the cattle were under control, and although not a man was hurt, they were a sorry bunch. The cattle had to be guarded, so there was little rest for any of them.

"During the day's work, the *vaqueros* changed mounts as

26

many as four times because their riding was hard. The cowmen held a high regard for their horses and would not exhaust them by riding them too long.

"There was always a *caballerango,* and for this rodeo Gabriel Anaya had the job. His duties were to drive the horses to the improvised corral which was enclosed by *reatas,* ropes. The horses were well trained, and it was seldom, if ever, that a horse tried to jump over the rope.

"Rafael Sánchez and Polo López had charge of the horses and when new mounts were wanted they roped the horses and the owner stood ready with the bridle in hand to put it on his horse. Each *vaquero* rode the horses which he claimed as his own and he usually had from seven to ten for *remuda,* change of mount. He may not have owned one, but a horse was as much a part of him as the pistol and holster which he never took off; his favorite was the cutting horse and his next best was his night horse.

"In order to have breakfast ready early, we had to start it the night before, so we buried a pot of beans and put our meat to barbecue. In the morning, we set Dutch ovens to heat while we made the dough for bread and started the coffee. We always had black coffee, as Santiago had remarked that morning.

"Some Easterner coming to New Mexico for the first time observed, 'In New Mexico there are more rivers and less water, and more cows and less milk than in any other country,' and he was right. We raise cows for beef; we cannot starve the calves in order to drink the milk.

"Before going to bed, I banked the fire and I hardly had gone to sleep when Señor Antonio's usual morning greeting started.

"The second day of the rodeo followed the same pattern as the first. Señor Antonio made his daily speech and the men under him swore at him with greater strength, only to do his bidding in the same humble way once they had their boots on.

"A few of the men went out to scour the country for any stray cattle, but the other men kept on with the branding as we did not finish that day or the next. It took a whole week to brand all the calves.

"That evening as we listened to the guitars and to the discussions of the men, Don Andrés turned to the men and asked, 'Why did we have such few calves to brand for Don Manuel today? I thought we sighted a large bunch of cows with his brand on the Mesa Rica as we came along two days ago.'

"Juan Arellano replied, 'We found the cows, *patrón,* but they were without calves; their udders were bursting with milk, so we know they had calves.'

" 'Thieves again,' murmured Don Andrés. 'We must look for tracks tomorrow and see if we cannot find the marauders.'

"He stood up and called, 'I want all of Don Manuel Salcedo's cowboys to come forward.'

"The word was passed on around the camp and all the men not on night duty stood before their *caporal.*

" 'Boys,' he said, 'Tomorrow you are not helping with the branding, you are going hunting for cattle rustlers. They cannot be very far and since unbranded calves are their loot, you cannot miss. All of you start at Mesa Rica, divide in pairs and follow all tracks leading to the four directions.'

" 'Be careful boys, I do not want any accidents, and do not shoot, unless it is in self-defense, for if the law is to be applied let it be done by the proper authorities.'

"Mauricio Sena came forward, 'I am to be *vigil,* on guard, at midnight, señor, could you send someone in my place?'

" 'I shall take your place as night rider tonight. Now all of you

28

go and get your rest, for you must be on your way before daybreak.'

"A sad bunch were Don Andrés' men as they started on a mission, which all the cowboys knew might end in tragedy, and, as they left that morning, all the men wished them good luck and Godspeed.

"Six days elapsed and the men were ready to move camp to the Rio Colorado country. Many of the cowboys had gone ahead to announce the coming of the rodeo so that other men might join the outfit.

"The camp moved slowly, traveling about twenty miles each day, for remember there were no roads and the wagons moved with difficulty over the rough beargrass (yucca) country.

"The rodeo camp consisted of two wagons and about a hundred head of horses. The chuck wagon, which Señor Antonio and I drove, carried the food and the few cooking utensils. The hoodlum's wagon, which was driven by a flunky, carried the bedrolls, branding irons, ammunition and guns.

"When the men of each outfit finished branding its herds, they left the rodeo group and departed for their headquarters.

"The last night in each place was spent in bidding adieu to friends and making promises of meeting at a fiesta, *baile* (dance), or the next rodeo, so there was a great deal of merrymaking to make up for the time when work put them to bed early.

"As I said before, there were plenty of musicians and singers to make the evening gay. The storytellers were always popular and when the men tired of music, they surrounded the storytelling group.

"Tales of buffalo hunts were very popular by those having followed the trail into the Ceja and the Llano. Usually the storytellers were old men who no longer rode the range but served as cooks, *caballerangos,* or guides.

"Señor Antonio soon called to the men, 'If we can make good time, tomorrow we can reach San Hilario in time for the evening preparation for the fiesta.' *'Sí* señores,' Alejo sighed. 'The lovely señoritas there are worth a day's hard ride.' 'To bed and let's dream about them,' chimed in several voices.

"Long before daybreak, Señor Antonio had the camp moving. We reached the Gallegos ranch by sunup and the men stopped there long enough to eat breakfast and to be joined by Don Jesús María's cowboys.

"To our surprise, we were met by four of Don Andrés' men who had left us four days before. One of the men had his arm in a sling, and his head bandaged.

"Señor Andrés came forward and asked, 'Did you catch up with the thieves?'

" 'Yes, sir,' answered Juan Arellano. 'We followed their trail into the Mesa Rica where we surprised them at their camp on the Venado Spring. It was a hard fight, for they were well prepared, but by strategy we caught every one of them. Manuel Quintana was slightly wounded. We would have taken the law in our hands and the thieves would be hanging by their necks, but we decided that they would suffer more if we tied them up and took them on to Puerto de Luna to be tried. Rafael and Juanito are taking care of them and the other boys are driving the calves, which they had not killed, back to their mothers.'

" 'Did you brand the calves?' asked Señor Andrés.

" 'Yes, we did, we stopped at San Lorenzo for help.'

"The caravan continued on its way, being joined by different outfits all along the way to San Hilario."

4. Fiesta at San Hilario

THE FIRST PEAL OF THUNDER made us aware of the approaching rain, but the storm was still thirty miles away.

El Cuate seemed not to have heard. He was far away in the days of Spanish fiestas and as the lightning brightened the *ambiente* around us, he continued with his tale:

"In San Hilario, they were expecting the rodeo. We had made good time and arrived there on Santiago's eve, and as the last bell was ringing for Vespers in the Chapel of San Hilario, our group reached the outskirts of the village.

"This chapel was built by Don Hilario Gonzáles, who had long since passed away. Don Hilario, in his day, ran more cattle on the Llano than we had gathered in our rodeo at Carrizito; his wagons traveling from the plains to Las Vegas were counted by the hundreds. May he rest in peace!

"In San Hilario on that day ruled another *patrón,* and I reckon there must have been at least twenty families there. The *patrón* with his sons and daughters, their children and the *empleados,* employees, with their families, made up the settlement, the latter being as much a part of the family as the children of the *patrón.*

"Every man, woman, and child in the village, as well as families from the surrounding plazas, had gathered in the church for Vesper service. Bonfires were burning around the church.

31

"The sound of singing reached our camp and the boys who were more devout, or those who had reached the age when salvation seemed important, joined the procession which was already forming.

"While Señor Antonio and I started the meal, the boys were making preparations for the *baile* which followed Vespers. We knew there would be few boys there to eat but it was a matter of habit to prepare food.

"On stacks of bedrolls, there were men getting haircuts and shaves, for we had boys who were pretty good barbers; some were shaving themselves beside the wagon and others had gone to get a dip in the village ditch. Clean shirts, socks and underwear came out of knapsacks and *pronto,* the men were ready for the ball.

"I was not too old to enjoy whirling the pretty señoritas, and in those days, as today on the ranches, no one ever got too old to dance.

"You should have seen your papá then. It was his first dance as well as his first rodeo." (Papá only smiled as he puffed hard on his pipe. He was more interested in the rain just then.)

"By eight o'clock, the dance hall was filled and the *baile* had started.

"First came the march in which everyone took part, husbands, wives, brothers and sisters, and some daring young fellows with their sweethearts danced together.

"The musicians with their violins, guitars and accordions were seated on a platform. Ramón Atencio, Francisco Anaya, Juan Romero, Agustín Sena and Manuel Ortega had come from San Lorenzo to play for the dance.

"After the march, the *bastonero,* the master of ceremonies, took charge, and only those whom he called could get a partner for the dances that followed. As a sign of courtesy to visitors, one of our men, Felipe Tafoya, was chosen as the *bastonero*. He was partial to your papá, and were the señoritas glad! For his first dance, your papá certainly danced like a professional.

"It was the custom, when anyone danced for the first time, to take the person and carry him in arms around the hall. This was called the *amarre*. Before he was allowed to go, someone close in friendship or relationship had to redeem him. This redemption was the *desempeño*. The *desempeño* usually was a promise of a dance at a fixed date. Juan María Quintana, your grandfather's *caporal,* came to your papá's rescue by promising a dance on San Lorenzo's day, the tenth of August, as we had hoped to reach San Lorenzo with the rodeo on that date.

"There were many beautiful señoritas at the dance and good dancers as well. The girls were well chaperoned and it was not easy for lovers to have much opportunity for love-making, yet they managed, and after one of these *bailes,* the families of many prospective grooms went in search of brides for their sons. It was still the custom for the parents to make matches, but American influence was becoming more and more evident as the years rolled on, and the young folks were more at liberty to choose their mates.

"The dance was a beautiful sight. The señoritas in voluminous skirts, tight waists and elegant jewelry, were swung around by the cowboys of two languages, in fancy boots, bright shirts and bandannas. The tiny feet of the women were lost in the fast rhythm of the polkas, schottisches, waltzes and varsovianas, and only the boots could be seen and heard.

"The boys from our camp and others who were joining the rodeo at this point, kept assembling for the merrymaking. They were greeted and welcomed by the men of the village as they came in, with the usual greeting of how are your parents and your family, or your *patrón,* heard with every new arrival. The ever-important questions of have you had much rain down your way and how was the calf crop this year, were asked of each one.

"As the dance continued, the conversation was kept up by the older men with an occasional drink. They discussed the weather, cattle bogged down in the creeks and water holes, cattle rustling, packs of wolves attacking the stock, marriages, deaths. Such were the stories exchanged by people hungry for outside social contact in those days of limited communication.

"During the dance those who had prestige with the *bastonero,* would choose the piece to their liking and soon the *músicos* were striking a polka or waltz and putting as much fervor in it as the dancers on the floor.

"As the musicians struck the first waltz, the audience looked around to see who had requested it. The first couple on the floor was the answer: Narciso Paez had Rosa Salcedo in his arms. Every eye was upon them. The couple seemed to have been made for each other and as they waltzed and waltzed, they seemed to be in a world all of their own, quite oblivious of the crowd around them.

"Doña María Inez de Salcedo drew her rebozo to her face as if to hide for her daughter the gaze of the crowd.

"Everyone for miles around the country, knew that Narciso and Rosa were in love with each other, but the match did not please Don Manuel Salcedo, only because Narciso's father was a poor man according to Don Manuel's way of reckoning wealth. The Paezes had less money, but better blood than the Salcedos.

"This has nothing to do with my story, but I cannot help but mention it, as I can never recall that rodeo without thinking of the tragedy which happened as we wound up in Revuelto in September.

"When the dance was over, one by one the boys came back to camp to rest from the long day's travel and a night of pleasure. I watched Narciso as he lay on his bed; he had that far away look which had seemed to accompany him since he became of a marriageable age.

"In those days, dances broke up at daylight for those who came long distances had to wait for daylight to travel home. It became a custom, even when people were remaining for the feast the following day.

"By ten o'clock next morning the bells were ringing to call the people to hear Mass in honor of Santiago, and every home was open to guests and prepared to feed anyone who would share its hospitality.

"Señor Antonio and I knew there was no use preparing a meal, so we joined the crowds in the village and partook of Don Juan Peña's hospitality, for there were no social lines drawn as to who should sit at the hosts' tables. Everyone was treated alike. The men were fed first; I do not know when the women ate.

"In the afternoon we had horse races, bronco riding, and the cock race.

"The boys saddled their most vicious horses and gave performances of their skill, for there were the señoritas, each watching to see how brave was the man of her heart. Often a cowboy lost his seat and landed on *tierra firme,* provoking a great deal of mirth.

"The cock race was the main event, because San Hilario and San Lorenzo were competing for the *corrida,* or run. This sport, like all sports, was colorful as well as cruel. Six live roosters had been buried head down in the ground midway between the two villages. The opposite teams, on horses trained for the game, were ready to start. A shot was fired to send off the cock racers. They

35

dug their spurs into their horses and off they went. The leader of San Hilario contestants was off before the spectators had time to focus their eyes on him. The San Lorenzo contestants pursued him and at every quarter of a mile a *mampuesto,* or guard, was ready to take the *gallo* away from him. The successful rider with horse foaming at its mouth and covered with beady sweat, reached the plaza while the other contenders were struggling with the *mampuestos* all along the way. As I remember, the San Hilario team took four roosters and was declared winners.

"The excited people cheered and shouted. The men and even the women had large wagers on the *corrida,* and it was a long while before the enthusiasm broke down.

"After a night and day of merrymaking, we were ready to retire, but not a boy was fit to do any work on the morrow. The rodeo must continue and again next morning we listened to Señor Antonio's daily sermon.

"We spent ten days in San Hilario and then moved on to San Lorenzo. San Lorenzo had been the home of the López family. Don Francisco López had the most beautiful daughters I have ever seen. Those of my class could only look at them, but there were pretty girls in my class too, only we always like to touch forbidden objects to see if they are real. Don Francisco had long been dead and his family scattered throughout New Mexico, but in the village their influence still could be felt.

"This was to be your papá's dance of *desempeño* and Juan María Quintana was not one to be outdone. He had sent a messenger to Las Vegas to bring the best of musicians and they were there when we arrived in San Lorenzo, but your papá can tell you about that dance."

Papá did not show any interest, as he never discussed his love affairs or youthful sprees before his children.

36

THE first drops of rain began to be felt, so the audience quickly moved into the house, much to my chagrin. It might be years before El Cuate would be in the mood for storytelling again.

But no, El Cuate seemed to have his mind on the story which he had been telling, for as we sat in the house he remarked:

"Who would now believe that there had been gay and happy plazas on the Llano?"

I took advantage of his word, and to start him off again I asked, "What was the tragedy in Revuelto about which you spoke as you told about the *baile?*"

It was like winding a clock, and El Cuate started with greater interest.

"By September the rodeo reach Revuelto ready to wind up the season.

"We had made San Rafael, Saladito, Plaza Larga. Each of these had their chapels, but we missed the patron saints' feasts of San Rafael, Nuestro Padre Jesús, and Santo Niño. Nevertheless in each place the rodeo crowd was welcomed with a dance.

"The boys were retiring after the *baile*. I had been in bed for several hours, and although when I went to bed, I missed Narciso Paez' mount, I gave it no thought, for he had been at the dance early in the evening.

"The boys were whispering among themselves as they lay on their beds, but I thought they were telling about their conquests at the *baile*.

"In the morning before Señor Antonio's voice started, I heard galloping hoofs approaching. Tito Lucero came towards my bed. I could not see him, but I knew every boy by instinct. Because he dismounted, I knew something was not well, so I asked: 'What happened, Tito?' He and Narciso were inseparable. He could not talk, he only lay his head on my shoulder and wept. This relieved

37

him and he spoke. 'Narciso is dead. He was shot by Don Manuel. He and Rosa were eloping.'

"I made some coffee as quickly as was possible over a campfire. The boys did not have to be awakened by Señor Antonio, for all had heard Tito's horse. Before the coffee boiled, they were getting the details from him.

"Felipe Tafoya, who was always strong tempered, cried, 'We shall lynch that old tyrant,' and he meant it. Señor Andrés came forward and said, 'Be careful boys, I know how you feel. We all loved Narciso but we cannot bring him back to life by revenge or any other means, and I know he would not have wanted any of you boys to stain your hands with blood. The law will take its course.'

" 'The rodeo is breaking up, and those of you who wish to pay respects to the Paez family can move to San Rafael.'

"The whole rodeo traveled to San Rafael; we were all there to bury our pal."

"What became of Rosa?" I asked.

El Cuate, brushing a tear, replied, "Don Manuel took her home and forbade her to leave the house, but the servants said that he need not have done that, because life for Rosa was buried in the San Rafael graveyard. On the south side of the chapel a cross marks Narciso's grave. The people there told that, after dark, a ghost appeared each year on the eve of San Rafael, while the merrymakers were reveling at the *baile*. Some said it was not a ghost, but Señorita Rosa who would ride from San Hilario to cry at her lover's grave. She and Narciso had danced together for this feast since they were children.

"Don Manuel was a broken man after that, but since he was a powerful man, only his daughter knew for sure who had murdered her lover."

38

5. Buffalo Hunters

THE RAIN KEPT COMING DOWN IN TORRENTS, as it often does on the Llano. We pray for rain and when it comes we get full value for our prayers; then we wish it would be portioned over a period of months instead of one night. But we are happy to see it come when it does.

Listening to El Cuate tell of early life on the Llano brought memories of my childhood and of stories which I had heard when I was so young that I already had forgotten. I remembered we had a dried buffalo hide on which Señor Ramón pounded the wool of our matresses each housecleaning season. I had grown up with the hide as a possession in our home, but what history it might have concealed had never bothered me. Tonight I became curious to learn about the buffaloes that once had roamed even where our ranch house stood.

El Cuate being so generous tonight, I knew we could stay up until Papá went to bed, and that would not happen until he had seen the last drop drained from the clouds.

"Cuate," I said, "You mentioned that you and Alejo Padilla had been *ciboleros*. Did you hunt for buffalo here on the Carrizito?"

"I cannot say that it happened right here, but often when we passed the Pajarito Creek, we saw some stragglers. We were always glad to sight them, for after the long trip from Las Vegas, which took several days, we were hungry for fresh meat. We never let one animal get away from us and we killed these stragglers to feed our caravans.

"The *cíbolos,* buffaloes, were migratory. In the spring they would graze north as far as the Canadian border and in the late summer and fall would wander south as far as the big bend of the Rio Grande where it dashes to its mouth on the Gulf of Mexico. In the latter part of October the herds, which numbered thousands and thousands, would be seen crossing the Canadian river, and in the vicinity of Los Barrancos Amarillos (Amarillo, Texas) the animals would tarry until the weather turned so cold that the blizzards drove them further south.

"After the harvest in the settlements along the Rio Grande and Pecos rivers were finished, the *ciboleros,* the buffalo hunters, started their march towards the Llano. Each village had a *cibolero* and a trained horse, or perhaps two, for the hunt. These horses were guarded with care and never used for any other purpose but the buffalo hunt.

"I do not remember the day of the *carretas,* but my father went to the *cíbolos* when only *carretas* were used for loading the meat. In my day, we had wagons which were pulled by oxen.

"Caravans of ten to thirty wagons were formed from the different villages; each wagon pulled by four or five yokes of oxen. It was a beautiful sight to see these processions on the march. There were burros and mules, and these belonged to the men who went along as *agregados,* assistants. Being poor, I went along as an *agregado.* Our job was to help skin the animals and to cut the meat into strips to make *tasajo,* jerky. We were too poor to organize a caravan of our own, so we were glad to be allowed to join as helpers and in that way secure meat for our families. Our share we loaded on our burros or mules to carry home.

40

"When the caravan was organized, one man was made *mayordomo* or *comandante,* and he had full control of the outfit. His word was law.

"We traveled very slowly, for the roads were bad and the oxen moved at a turtle's pace. It took about two weeks to make the trip from Las Vegas to Palo Duro Canyon and the Quitaque Country.

"As we traveled along, we met other caravans on the way, and when we reached the bluffs of the Llano Estacado, the Staked Plains, we were many companies. Some were already there and it became a small world, this big land of New Mexico.

"On reaching the buffalo country, the caravans pitched camp. The hunt would not start at midday, if we happened to reach the hunting grounds at that time. We made preparations by getting the horses and hunters ready. At daybreak the hunters from the different outfits gathered together, mounted their prancing steeds and off they went towards the herd. The hunters used no saddle, only a pad on the horse's back. This protected the rider from tangling in the stirrups if he fell off the horse. The hunters used lances five or six feet long made of the finest steel.

"The hunters formed a group before dashing into the herd, bowed their heads in prayer and invoked Santiago, the patron saint of Spain, to help them and guide them in the hunt. After making the sign of the cross, into the herd they rode, jabbing their lances inside the left ribs of choice fat animals, directly into the heart. A run, or *corrida,* usually would be three miles, during which each hunter killed from fifteen to twenty-five animals. This number was sufficient for one day, as they had to be skinned and the meat cut up for jerky. It was a full day's work, and I know, for when dusk came we were ready for rest. The *agregados* and the *carreros,* wagon drivers, followed the hunters into the herd to pick up the carcasses and bring them into camp. We had one man in each crew who was an expert in bleeding the animals, and he always was ahead of the crew."

"Why didn't you use guns for hunting, Cuate?" I asked.

"In the early days, the firearms of the Spaniard were of the musket type and they were not very effective. The early Spanish hunters learned from the Indian that the lance was the swiftest method, and being fond of excitement, they found that hunting with a lance was real sport and that it took much valor to pursue it.

"We enjoyed hunting the buffalo, and had not the *Americanos* come in with their guns, we might still be enjoying the sport, but it did not take them long with their rifles to clear the Llano of buffaloes.

"In the camps there was great activity—the meat had to be cared for quickly or it would spoil. The *agregados* cut the meat into strips. Some of the hides were cut into strips to be used as lines on which to hang the meat for drying. When the meat was dry, it was placed on the wagon beds and tramped down so that the wagon could be loaded to full capacity. It took four yokes of oxen to pull one of the heavy wagons. The fat was rendered into tallow to be used for cooking and for making candles.

"We had many uses for the hides. Some were made into *reatas,* ropes, and others were tanned with the hair left on them for robes or rugs.

I knew, then, the hide we used for pounding the mattress wool must have been a discarded robe or rug, but I did not interrupt El Cuate, for the story was becoming more and more fascinating.

He continued, "We plucked the wool from the buffaloes' shoulders and necks; this was used for filling mattresses and it also was spun into cloth.

"We remained in the buffalo country for a long time and when we were ready to leave, it was cold enough so that we could carry fresh meat in our wagons to supply our tables during cold weather.

"With wagons and pack animals loaded, we were a happy bunch of *ciboleros,* saying *adios, hasta el año venidero.* We headed west to our homes along the rivers and to our mountain habitations to spend a good winter well supplied with meat. We said, *hasta luego*—but there came a day when we did not return because the wonderful sport had vanished. We have only the tales to remind us of when the Llano belonged to the Indian and to the New Mexicans of Spanish descent. Ballads are still sung in the villages about the *cíbolos* and the *ciboleros,* but never again

43

will the colorful processions be seen where the Hispanos and the Comanches met in friendly terms.

"I have heard you children sing the *corrido* about Manuel Maes. Manuel was one of the best buffalo hunters, for a young man, that I ever knew, but it was his fate to die while pursuing his beloved sport. It was in 1863 the tragedy occurred, and those of us who witnessed it shall never forget. Manuel was riding a horse which was not yet broken for the chase. As Maes went to thrust his lance into a buffalo cow, his horse shied from another buffalo and plunged towards the animal he was about to kill. The lance slipped from Manuel's hand, turning completely around with the butt end hitting against the buffalo he was aiming toward. The impact and the horse plunging toward the animal caused the lance to pierce Manuel's body. We were hunting where the city of Amarillo stands today. Manuel was buried there on the Llano, and today his grave remains unknown and unmarked, with perhaps a wheatfield waving over it.

"I have told you about the hunting of the buffalo, but I must not pass up telling you something about the animals.

"The animals were huge; they stood about six feet high and they had a ferocious look on their hairy faces. When we sighted a herd, they appeared like a black cloud in the distance.

"As a rule, the buffalo was a very stupid animal and not only men helped to destroy him, but, just as our cattle perished from droughts, prairie fires and snows, likewise the buffaloes died.

"The wolf was the buffalo's deadly enemy. The bulls were the protectors of the herd, but it did not take much to frighten them, and one would have cows and calves in one's power.

"Some of the horses were deathly afraid of the bulls, especially if they had experienced a stampede. A buffalo stampede was much more to be dreaded than one of cattle. I once saw a herd

44

stampede over a cliff and every head was killed as they fell into a deep canyon. I was so impressed by the tragedy, that, for a day, I could not join the *agregados* in skinning the animals and getting my share of the meat.

"Sometimes we lingered on the Llano until winter, for the hides were worth more when they were covered thickly with hair. Hunting in winter was almost sure death for some of the hunters. The snows and winds on the Llano chill a man clear into his intestines. The Llano furnished no protection for man or beast. Alejo Padilla used to tell about a hunter who was lost in a snowstorm. They had been hunting all day when the storm set in. The hunter removed the entrails from a buffalo which he had killed. He crawled inside the carcass for protection and during the night the carcass froze solid, making the hunter a captive. Alejo and some of his companions went to search for him, and, luckily for him, they heard his cries. After much work they thawed out the carcass but the man himself had to be thawed out too. He fared pretty well, for considering the plight in which he had been, he only lost one arm and was forever more known as 'El Manco.'

"In the days of the buffalo, the lobos, the prairie wolves, followed the herds. Once in a while they killed a straggler, but mostly they lived on carrion, the dead buffaloes left by the hunters who killed the animals for the skins. After the buffaloes were exterminated, the lobos moved into the Ceja.

"They followed herds of sheep and looked for a chance to kill. A lobo was never contented unless he killed wholesale. A lobo would not start eating until it had killed and stripped from twenty-five to fifty head.

"About 1880, some cowboys from the S-T lassoed a lobo pup

on the Mesa Redonda. They put a bell on it and turned it loose. The sheepherders hearing the bell would think it was a *corta,* a stray bunch of sheep, and many a day they spent looking for sheep and sometimes sighted the lobo. The lobo traveled over the Llano country, he was now seen on Mesa Rica, on Luciano Mesa, or around the Alamogordo country. It was a menace to the herds, killing many sheep. The sheep were not afraid of it because of the bell—they were accustomed to the sound of bells on sheep. As the years rolled on, the lobo became a subject of superstition among the herders, and no one would dare kill it. Many heroic feats were attributed to the lobo with the bell over the Llano land. After about six years of roaming and killing, the animal was killed by Don Juan José Quintana on the Chirisco, and thus ended a cowboy prank created to scare the sheepherders and try to end the sheep industry in the feud between cattlemen and sheepmen.

"*Si,* señores, those were the days. There were no cattle rustlers because meat was plentiful, but it took courage to face the dangers of the Llano."

6. Comancheros

WE ALL STAYED UP THAT NIGHT until the rain started to come down gently. We heard Carrizito Creek roaring like a mad bull, so we were sure that we had been blessed with a good downpour and we knew that when the downpour ceased and a gentle rain set in, we would have a two or three day drencher.

El Cuate told us he was tired, but promised to tell us about the Comanches on the morrow, for he was sure we would have to stay in the house. And, just as we thought, the next day was drizzly. The boys, with slickers on, went out as a matter of habit but soon returned to the family circle by the kitchen fire.

El Cuate started to reminisce about torrential and drizzly rains which he had experienced and somehow wandered to his Comanche tales:

"The Comanche Indians had been friendly with the *ciboleros* for more than a century. As we traveled into the Ceja and the Llano to hunt for buffalo, we carried with us bread, *panocha*— sprouted wheat pudding, whiskey, guns, cotton fabrics, beads, knives, and other articles. These we traded with our friends, the Comanches.

"The Comanches resented the moving of the Texans and other stockmen with their cattle into their land. Stealing cattle

47

was the means of revenge which the Indians used against the cattle owners. The Comanches would meet us at our camps along the buffalo country. There we exchanged our goods for cattle and horses that the Indians had driven from the unfenced land of the cattle kings. We gained very little from the trade, as the Americans to whom we sold the cattle paid us low prices for them. It was merely getting rid of them for whatever we could get. The leading New Mexican *patrones,* who sent their wagons for the buffalo hunt, did not approve of our dealings with the Comanches. They looked upon us *Comancheros* as common cattle thieves.

"Our secret meeting places and dealings were unknown to those for whom we worked.

"Don Hilario Romero, who was sheriff of San Miguel county in the days of illicit trade, was instrumental in stopping a great deal of the Comanche traffic; he aided the *Tejanos,* the Texans, in recovering many of their cattle and at the same time kept them from driving stock that did not belong to them—for when they came to recover their cattle, they would drive every cow which was in their path.

"The *Americanos* around us were the real racketeers in the business. They did the buying from us, then they would drive the loot to Colorado, Kansas, Nebraska, or to California where they sold it at great profit. Very few of the stolen cattle ever were kept in New Mexico.

"I knew an American trader whose ranch was located at Aguilar, a settlement between Chaperito and Antonchico. He did a big business with the *Comancheros.* The cattle owners, from over the line, found out about him and soon were on his trail. He was always alert to strangers seen in his pasture, and this was lucky for him, for when he got wind of being trailed, he took to the hills and kept in hiding in Chupaina Mesa. The *Tejanos* recovered about fifteen hundred head of cattle with their brands but not without a fight. The cowboys hired by the *Americano* brought out their guns and there was real war. The *Tejanos* were victorious and besides recovering their cattle, they took one of the cowboys of the *Americano* and lynched him. They left him hanging from a pine tree close to the house.

"In trading with the Comanches, we rounded up the cattle at night by the light of the moon and we drove them on a fast run. We made thirty miles by daylight. We left the bulls, weak cows and calves behind, as they could not keep up with the herd. A party of Comanche Indians would stay behind to fight and hold the *Tejanos* back in case of pursuit.

"The American Government kept on the trail of the Comanches, but often the officers who were sent out to stop the illicit trade found it profitable to engage in it themselves and thus delayed the end of it for several years.

"By 1876 the trade began to wane, and the Comanches, who were finally rounded up by the military government, were put on reservations. So ended a colorful business which remains only as a happy memory of our meeting with our friends the Comanches in Palo Duro Canyon, Canyon de Tule, Tierra Blanca, Río de Las Lenguas, and the Valle de Lágrimas.

"AFTER the Indians no longer roamed the Llano and the Comanche trade died out, I went to work for John Chisum, a big cattle owner in the lower Pecos valley. I made trips to Bosque Redondo, where the Navajos had been put on a reservation, to deliver meat to the government for my *patrón*. There I served as interpreter between the American officers and the Indians. Juan Anaya, father of Chee Dodge, spoke Navajo and Spanish. I spoke English and Spanish. Juan Anaya, who was of Hispano extraction, had been captured by the Navajos when he was a child and he grew up among them as one of the tribe. His son, Chee Dodge, a great man among his people, became well known and highly respected for his wisdom. Juan Anaya, in his time, was also a great leader.

"Gradually the buffalo disappeared, and on the Llano land the grass grew without disturbance. The Indians no longer roamed the country to endanger the lives of those who saw promise for good grazing on the Comanche domain. Cattle companies began to push forward and the New Mexican sheepman and small cattleman, who was usually a lone owner, could not hold out against the powerful syndicates. The war was on between two contenders, neither of whom had a deed to the land.

"The early livestock man had not needed fences, but the incoming cattle companies started building them. The New Mexicans were ready to fight for the land which traditionally had been theirs, and out of this grew up an organization of influential New Mexicans for protection against the usurpers. These citizens banded together and, by cutting down a few fences, discouraged fence building by those who had no titles for the land. Perhaps the building of fences had not been the main reason for the New Mexicans becoming irate. The cowboys of the cattle companies drove and killed sheep right and left, whipped the sheepherders and made plenty of trouble in other ways.

"Your grandfather, who was then running sheep in the Plaza Larga country, brought to trial a bunch of cowboys who had killed several hundred of his sheep. The cowboys were prosecuted, but the country was too vast for all the sheepmen to catch up with the marauders."

50

III. PLACES
& PEOPLE

7. Chapels on the Llano

AS A CHILD, I LIVED WITH MY PATERNAL GRANDPARENTS on their hacienda across the Gallinas river from the village of La Liendre, eighteen miles southeast of Las Vegas. This, our ancestral home, was the stopping place for all who made trips into the Ceja and the Llano to oversee their large sheep and cattle holdings. In this environment, the history of the country was imprinted on my mind from early childhood.

My grandfather, Don Tomás Cabeza de Baca, with the help of the Chaperito and La Liendre villagers and his *empleados,* financed the building of a toll road over Vega Hill into Las Vegas in the early 1870's. The climb over this hill had been a treacherous one for travelers. Las Vegas was the trading center for all the country from West Texas, Puerto de Luna and Fort Sumner to the lower Pecos territory. The wagons were a continuous caravan over this road, and it was a good day when they could travel over a graded hill, although it was still a pretty steep ascent. The road was kept up by one man who lived at the foot of the climb and who collected the toll fee of twenty-five cents for each vehicle.

No better-known character than Señor Mariano Urioste will be remembered as the tollkeeper. This lonely soul could tell more stories of Indian raids, cattle thieves, and buffalo hunts than any other man of his time. Every wagon had to rest its horses or

51

mules before starting the hard climb, and Señor Mariano was happy to play host to all the travelers. In his tiny hut, in the open fireplace, was an everlasting pot of boiling coffee.

Each traveler, Señor Mariano would make welcome by saying, "Come my children, drink a cup of coffee, merely the boiled grounds, but my heart goes with it. I can do without it, but you are traveling." The voyager would, naturally, accept the hospitality offered him, and in return would give him coffee and other provisions. Señor Mariano always had a full larder. No traveler ever left without hearing who had gone ahead and what stories had been picked up by Señor Mariano. He was the radio and newspaper from the 1880's until as late as 1912, when the state started road building and the traffic was routed over Cañon del Agua Hill.

Our home at La Liendre was a modern two-story structure. Every room had a fireplace with ornate black moulding. The house was built on a hill and below it were the orchard, the well which supplied us with domestic water, a large cottonwood and poplar park, with the Gallinas river running close by. The village was across the river and most of the men worked for grandfather on the farm and others were on the Ceja with the sheep and cattle.

One of the most pleasant memories I have is of the ruins of the old house which my grandparents had occupied when they first moved to La Liendre from Las Vegas in 1870. It was similar to the ones built by the *ricos* in Santa Fe, Las Vegas and other towns in earlier days.

The people who traveled into the Ceja and Llano and who stopped with us on their way to their ranches or to the plazas, had lived in homes similar to ours, the old and the new, but their homes on the Llano were different.

The towns on the Llano were small, with the families of the *patrón* and his *empleados* making up the scattered settlements. The homes were not like the ones which they left behind; they were simple rock or adobe structures, because materials which were not native to the country had to be hauled from Las Vegas over rough mountain roads or trails—distances varying from fifty to two hundred miles. The chapels were not imposing edifices. They were unpretentious in architecture, built of the best materials available. The women dug deep into their trunks and chests to bring out laces, silk, gold and silver to adorn the interiors. From their ancestral homes, on the lower and upper Rio Grande and on the Pecos river, the colonists brought their favorite *santos.* These *santos,* religious statues and paintings, may have seen their origin in Spain, Mexico, or in the northern New Mexico villages—where local *santeros* may have been the artisans. These families who settled on the Llano were not of the poor classes; they were of the landed gentry, in whose veins ran the noble blood of ancestors who left the mother country, Spain, for the New World. The solid gold or silver chalices, the ornate satin vestments for the priests, and the handmade or handpainted *santos* were the gifts of the *patrón* and his family to their place of worship.

To the New Mexican of Spanish origin, his religion is his whole being. Everything is entrusted to God, with a faith so sincere and deep-rooted that it is hardly comprehensible to those not of the faith. The chapels were prepared with pomp for the coming of the priest. Each chapel or place of worship had a *mayordomo* for the year. Later it became customary to have two families as *mayordomos,* and the custom still persists in the smaller communities. These *mayordomos* were responsible for keeping up the chapel, but for the coming of the priest, everyone joined

53

in whitewashing the inside walls, in plastering the outside, in cleaning the yard, and in decorating the altar. The priest came to say Mass as often as the roads and time permitted—once a year, twice a year. San Miguel, Chaperito, Antonchico, Puerto de Luna in New Mexico and Trinidad in Colorado, the seats of the parishes, were many miles on horseback from the chapels on the Llano under their jurisdiction. Quite often, Mass was said in a room prepared for the occasion, for not every settlement had a chapel.

I can still remember, just after the coming of the railroad over the plains (1905), going many miles to hear Mass in private chapels of the *ricos*. It had never been my privilege to own a silk dress, and to see girls my age dressed in satins and taffetas, seemed like the fairly tales of princesses which I had read. Everyone was attired more elegantly than anyone I had ever seen in Las Vegas. It was truly a great event. Some of the families came one or two days before the priest's arrival, and all who came were the guests of the *patrón* and his family.

Before the Mass started and while the priest heard confessions, the people gathered outside the church and exchanged news which concerned their daily lives. Rain was always a popular subject and I cannot remember a time when ranchers did not discuss how dry or wet the season was at the time of their meeting.

The priest performed marriages, baptisms, and blessed religious objects. When Mass was over, then came the feast, and a feast it was, for each *patrón* would not let it be said that he was not a generous host. Food was plentiful and it would have been an insult to the host's hospitality for anyone to leave without partaking of his fare.

No fiesta of today can compare with the one when the priest

54

came to say his annual, quarterly and—later—monthly Mass. In the early days on the Llano, there were families who traveled two or more days by wagon or carriage covering from fifty to one hundred miles to their nearest place of worship.

Messages announcing the Mass, which might have been the celebration of the patron saint's feast, were sent by the *patrón* to the surrounding ranches and villages. Men on horseback were the bearers of the news, because for many years, Las Vegas was the only post office serving the Llano for hundreds of miles. Later, in the '70's, mail could be received at Liberty, a wild West town which disappeared after the coming of the railroad. It was not a town in the true sense of the word, but with its one store, several saloons and a few scattered houses, it served as a gathering point for news, if the families on the Llano cared to have mail addressed to them there. Liberty stood about five miles from the present site of Tucumcari. Mail was so uncertain that if something of great urgency had to be transacted, a man on horseback served the purpose better. He changed mounts at different ranches and picked up his own on the return trip.

Perhaps no other influence was as instrumental in the preservation of the faith as was the Order of Brothers of Our Father Jesus of Nazareth, commonly called "Penitentes." This society is believed to have come from the Third Order of Saint Francis of Assisi, called the Order of Penance by the Saint. Whatever its origin, it certainly has held an important part in the religion of the New Mexican people of Spanish extraction, who, as late as 1850 were being served from Durango, Mexico. At that time there were only ten priests administering the vast territory. It is evident that something must have held the people to the faith and in studying Penitente rules as written in their constitution, one cannot help but feel that the order had a hand in preserving

55

religious rites when priests were scarce. These Brothers spread throughout New Mexico and their influence on the Llano settlers cannot be ignored, for they were far from the parish seats, yet the Catholic religion retained its strength.

Under the articles of incorporation of the Society, they are organized to protect their order from ignorance, prejudice and persecution. The aims of the Society are: To obey Our Lord Jesus Christ; to profess, practice and spread the Roman Catholic faith under the guidance of the Pope, the local bishop and the pastors; to form a religious society that can own property, sue and be sued against; to resist defamation by word of mouth and in writing.

The preamble states that their constitution is intended to promote justice, peace, union and assistance to members. The first seven articles comment on the last words of Jesus on the Cross. They are members of the Mystical Body of Christ; they must ever be disposed to forgive their enemies; Mary is their Mother; prayer should be their support in time of affliction; they must thirst for justice and charity; envy, hatred and ill will must give place to justice and charity; they shall all be united in the charity of Christ.

If the organization has deteriorated in some of its phases, it is because cunning politicians have tried to use its strength for their personal gain. The true, simple Christian faith is still evident and one who participates with them in their nonsecret rites, cannot but feel inspired by the strong reverence which they have for their religion.

There has been a transition in their practices and this has been due to outside influences. Nevertheless, it is a fact that the strong adherents of the order have been responsible for law and order and the spiritual well-being in isolated, remote areas.

As I recall, some of the people who were guests at our home were trying hard to hold the land on which had grazed their sheep and cattle, but they were losing it fast to the homesteaders. Before my day, the large cattle companies had pushed them in and only a few were left over the Texas line.

Those who had large herds of cattle and sheep in the '70's and '80's had helped many a family in the Ceja and Llano to build up their flocks and herds through the *partido* contract.

Many of the smaller ranchers who lived along the Río Colorado and in Oldham County, Texas, had been *partidarios* of the López and Gonzáles families. *Partidarios* were ranchers who took either cattle or sheep on the shares. The customary deal was to take a certain number of animals of certain ages and at the end of five years return double the number of stock of the same ages as those taken on the shares.

I remember clearly my grandfather's *partidarios*. As security, the *partidario* had a responsible person sign the contract with him and the stock was always a part of the security.

Later—in my day—my father had *partidarios,* but it was a different system. In place of returning double the stock at the end of five years, the stock was taken for any number of years agreed by the parties. The *partidario* paid the owner each year twenty percent in calf crop of the number of cattle taken on the shares. This is not correctly called *partido,* or share, but it has never changed nomenclature, a holdover from the early system.

Until a few years ago, the few cattle which I had were held on the twenty percent basis, first by my brother-in-law, Albert Branch, later by my brother, Luis.

Before the coming of the large herds from Texas and other eastern points, and prior to 1880, sizable fortunes were made by the Hispanos on the Ceja and the Llano by taking sheep and cattle on *partido* contracts. The range, then, was free; grass and water were plentiful and the stock raisers had all the land they needed or desired for grazing.

There was abundant living on the Ceja and Llano from 1870 to the beginning of the twentieth century. The calves, lambs, wool, hides and pelts were brought to Las Vegas to exchange for food, clothing, household equipment and money. Over the Vega Hill came the wagonloads of produce from the ranches below the mountains and happy men returned to their families with their wagons loaded with their barter.

THE women on the Llano and Ceja played a great part in the history of the land. It was a difficult life for a woman, but she had made her choice when in the marriage ceremony she had promised to obey and to follow her husband. It may not have been her choice, since parents may have decided for her. It was the Spanish custom to make matches for the children. Whether through choice or tradition, the women had to be a hardy lot in order to survive the long trips by wagon or carriage and the separation from their families, if their families were not among those who were settling on the Llano.

The women had to be versed in the curative powers of plants and in midwifery, for there were no doctors within a radius of two hundred miles or more.

The knowledge of plant medicine is an inheritance from the Moors and brought to New Mexico by the first Spanish colonizers. From childhood, we are taught the names of herbs, weeds and plants that have curative potency; even today when we have doctors at our immediate call, we still have great faith in plant medicine. Certainly this knowledge of home remedies was a source of comfort to the women who went out to the Llano, yet their faith in God helped more than anything in the survival.

Every village had its *curandera* or *médica* and the ranchers rode many miles to bring the medicine woman or the midwife from a distant village or neighboring ranch.

Quite often, the wife of the *patrón* was well versed in plant medicine. I know that my grandmother, Doña Estéfana Delgado de Baca, although not given the name of *médica,* because it was not considered proper in her social class, was called every day by some family in the village, or by their *empleados,* to treat a child or some other person in the family. In the fall of the year, she went out to the hills and valleys to gather her supply of healing

59

herbs. When she went to live in La Liendre, there were terrible outbreaks of smallpox and she had difficulty convincing the villagers that vaccination was a solution. Not until she had a godchild in every family was she able to control the dreaded disease. In Spanish tradition, a godmother takes the responsibility of a real mother, and in that way grandmother conquered many superstitions which the people had. At least she had the power to decide what should be done for her godchildren.

From El Paso, Texas, she secured vaccines from her cousin, Doctor Samaniego. She vaccinated her children, grandchildren and godchildren against the disease. She vaccinated me when I was three years old and the vaccination has passed many doctors' inspections.

As did my grandmother, so all the wives of the *patrones* held a very important place in the villages and ranches on the Llano. The *patrón* ruled the *rancho,* but his wife looked after the spiritual and physical welfare of the *empleados* and their families. She was the first one called when there was death, illness, misfortune or good tidings in a family. She was a great social force in the community—more so than her husband. She held the purse strings, and thus she was able to do as she pleased in her charitable enterprises and to help those who might seek her assistance.

There may have been class distinction in the larger towns, but the families on the Llano had none; the *empleados* and their families were as much a part of the family of the *patrón* as his own children. It was a very democratic way of life.

The women in these isolated areas had to be resourceful in every way. They were their own doctors, dressmakers, tailors and advisers.

The settlements were far apart and New Mexico was a poor

territory trying to adapt itself to a new rule. The Llano people had no opportunity for public schools, before statehood, but there were men and women who held classes for the children of the *patrones* in private homes. They taught reading in Spanish and sometimes in English. Those who had means sent their children to school in Las Vegas, Santa Fe, or Eastern states. If no teachers were available, the mothers taught their own children to read and many of the wealthy ranchers had private teachers for their children until they were old enough to go away to boarding schools.

Doña Luisa Gallegos de Baca, who herself had been educated in a convent in the Middle West, served as teacher to many of the children on the Llano territory.

Without the guidance and comfort of the wives and mothers, life on the Llano would have been unbearable, and a great debt is owed to the brave, pioneer women who ventured into the cruel life of the plains, far from contact with the outside world. Most of them have gone to their eternal rest and God must have saved a very special place for them to recompense them for their contribution to colonization and religion in an almost savage country.

The few who remain have interesting stories to relate of their life on the endless Llano and over the Cap Rock. During a visit with Doña Jesusita García de Chávez and her sister-in-law Doña Lola Otero de García in Albuquerque, I heard many stories of the old days.

In 1898, Don Antonio Chávez was running sheep at Plaza Larga. Mrs. Chávez tells of her experiences on the Llano, and although now past eighty, she still remembers many incidents of her earlier days. Liberty, originally Tierra Blanca, was then a wild West frontier town, serving as a mail center to the Llano settlers.

There are many mentions in Western books of Black Jack Ketchum, the bandit who terrorized eastern New Mexico. Mrs. Chávez tells that in the summer of 1898, Black Jack and another companion held up and robbed the store at Liberty. The outlaws were masked and at the points of their guns made the proprietor of the store, Levi Herstein, and the bystanders in the store face the wall. While one man held his gun on them, the other committed the raid.

Black Jack and his companion left Liberty and took a southerly course. A posse of four men led by Herstein started on the trail of the bandits. The three other members of the squad were Juan Apodaca, Plácido Gurulé, and Merejildo Gallegos. After trailing the bandits for about thirty miles, the posse overtook them on the banks of Plaza Larga Creek, eight miles west of the present Quay, New Mexico, and a quarter of a mile from the Antonio Chávez ranch.

The bandits watered their horses at the Chávez well and Mrs. Chávez remembers that their horses were shod with rawhide shoes. They had several horses which carried the loot from the Herstein store.

While the outlaws were eating their lunch under a cottonwood tree, the posse made the mistake of not opening fire on the thieves while at a safe distance. Instead, they tried to take them alive.

The desperados, expert at defense, opened fire on their pursuers. Gallegos was killed in the first volley; Herstein fell from his horse wounded and was shot through the heart while begging for mercy. Juan Apodaca made a dash for the Chávez ranch amid a shower of bullets and managed to escape unhurt. Plácido Gurulé, who fell from his horse when the shooting started, played possum, and did such a good job of it, that the bandits shot at him once after he was down to make sure that he was dead. He was shot in the hip, but self preservation gave him courage not to stir, making believe he was a corpse. Gurulé lived to be an old man and humorously delighted in telling of his experience. He often stopped at our *rancho*.

Black Jack met his doom soon after. He was shot by the conductor on the Denver and Fort Worth Railroad after two successful holdups of the same train by his brother Sam. The bandit was hanged in Clayton after a brief trial in April, 1901.

Recalling the incidents of her early married life and her youth on the Llano, Mrs. Chávez said:

"It was in Las Salinas where we lived that the climax of the feud between the Hispanos and the Texans was reached. The Texans were pushing in with their cattle—the New Mexicans resented this. The animosity was a holdover from the Mexican war of 1846. One night, at a dance, a drunken Texan killed an Hispano. The dance became a battle for all. The Hispanos killed the Texan and from then on, the war was on between the two nationalities—until, one by one, the Hispanos crossed into New Mexico to be pushed farther on, or completely out, as the homesteaders began to take up the land." She did not remember the names of those involved.

CONCERNING stories of Indian raids, which I heard as a child, Don Miguel Benavídez, who lived his later years on the Llano country, had firsthand knowledge of Indian life. In 1849, when he was about seven years of age, he and an older brother were herding goats at Los Esteritos, near Dilia. A band of warring Indians dropped in on them at their camp and took them captive. His brother managed to escape, but Miguel was taken by the Indians to the Dakotas, where he lived for many years.

On a campaign, one of many in which he took part against American soldiers, Miguel managed to be rescued. He was taken to St. Louis, Missouri, where he lived with an officer and his family. There he was treated as one of their kin. Years later he was sent back to New Mexico in one of the wagons coming over the Santa Fe trail. I heard Don Miguel's tales when I lived at his brother's house while teaching my first country school.

As a small child on my grandfather's hacienda, I remember an old man who came regularly for his weekly ration of food and clothing—the *hacendados* in those days took care of the poor by providing them with food and clothing. Many poor people came to our home, but I remember Señor Antonio Trujillo, the old man, better than any of the others. He always rode a donkey and had a little boy walking by his side and a pack of dogs following. The people of the village told that he ate dog meat and that was the reason for his keeping so many dogs. They also said that Señor Antonio had learned to eat dog meat when he lived with the Indians.

One of the stories which Señor Antonio used to relate was about his captivity by the Arapahoes and his life with them. When he was a small child, Antonio lived in Taos. A band of Arapahoes came down upon the village and, after raiding the town, they killed several persons—among them Antonio's parents. They took Antonio with them into Montana. (Señor Antonio did not know what state, but by his descriptions grandfather knew it must be the Montana area). He lived with the Indians until he was a grown man. While he was among the Arapahoes, he married a squaw. One night there was an Indian dance which his wife refused to attend. At a very late hour, after the dance was over, Antonio returned to their tepee, where his wife was soundly sleeping. He saw his chance for escape, and knowing that the tribe had no suspicion but that he was one of them, he decided to take flight. Cautiously, he pulled a *reata* from under his wife's pillow and quietly went out to the enclosure where the horses were corralled. There he picked two of the best horses and started on his journey. He crossed many high sierras and although pursued, he finally succeeded in reaching a French trading post. The trappers were very kind to him and helped to hide him for several days while his pursuers were on the trail. The Frenchmen afforded protection for him in a secret room and when there seemed to be no more danger, Antonio continued to travel. After many months of hardship, he reached Taos, being guided all the way by trappers.

Later he followed the buffalo trails and remained on the Llano, finally settling at La Liendre, where he died at the age of 105 years. He served as a soldier in the Spanish and Mexican armies and later fought for the North in the Civil War.

FEW of the chapels remain on the Llano. As one travels on the paved highways, ruins of once colorful villages, of ranch houses and chapels, are there to remind us of fiestas, gay pastoral life, and history which I have tried to gather.

The Hispano has almost vanished from the land and most of the chapels are nonexistent, but the names of hills, rivers, arroyos, canyons and defunct plazas linger as monuments to a people who pioneered into the land of the buffalo and the Comanche. These names have undergone many changes, but are still known and repeated. Very likely many of those who pronounce them daily are unaware that they are of Spanish origin.

Amarillo was named Los Barrancos Amarillos, the yellow cliffs. Arroyo de Trujillo was named after the family who founded the plaza. Atascosa, boggy land, is today called Tascosa. Cabra Spring was named so because travelers sighted wild goats in its vicinity. Cañon de Tule, bulrush canyon, has been abbreviated to Tule and even spelled Tool. Conchas, meaning shells, was so named because shells are found along the river shores.

Corazón Peak took its name because its shape resembles a heart. Cuervo is the Spanish word from crow, and the creek received the name from the abundance of crows in that area. La Liendre was originally settled by a family who were small in stature, whose nickname was *liendre,* meaning nit. Las Salinas were the salt mines. Los Alamitos signifies little cottonwoods. Luciano Mesa was named for a man whose given name was Luciano—he lived close to the mesa. Nara Visa was called Narvaez, after the family of that name. Nueve Millas, nine miles, was that distance from Plaza Larga.

We have Ojo del Carnero, sheep spring, named that because of wild sheep that came to water there; Ojo del Llano was a spring well-known on the Llano; Arroyo de Pajarito, little bird

66

creek, is an old landmark. Palo Duro is hardwood, after the hackberry trees growing in the area. Palomas was the name given to that mesa because of the doves which inhabited it. Pintada Mesa received its name because of the varied colors of the earth; it means painted tableland. Plaza Larga, long town, was called thus because of the many eroded buttes having the semblance of houses; these were in long stretches which gave the country the appearance of a city. Saladito means salty and indicated the saline quality of the creek.

Tierra Blanca, white earth, has been shortened to Blanca. Tucumcari is a Comanche word meaning woman's breast; the peak received its name because of resemblance to a well-rounded breast. Ceja means eyebrow, and it was called that because the woody vegetation formed an eyebrow over the endless Llano. The Canadian River, which the early French trappers called after their own country, had been named Rio Colorado or Rio Almagre by the Spaniards from its red mud coloring. Many other sonorous names remind us of a vanished people. Zanjon, translated deep gully, is today called San Jon, a change which would amuse the early buffalo hunters if they were to travel over the Llano again.

The Llano of today is populated: large towns, villages and ranches dot the country where the endless sea of grass, yucca and mesquite bushes so cruelly greeted the buffalo hunters and Comanche fighters. Cotton, wheat, maize and other grains grow in abundance on the Llano Estacado.

When the cattle companies and the homesteaders arrived, it was the survival of the fittest. Much of the land had reverted to the United States government. It was No Man's Land. The Llano became a cattle and farming country and a few foresighted Hispanos abandoned sheep and took to cattle raising on a small scale.

8. Sheep on a Thousand Hills

AFTER THE INDIANS WERE ROUNDED UP and put into reservations, it became safe for the sheepmen to take their families into the Ceja and Llano country.

Families from Las Vegas, Mora, Antonchico, some from the lower Rio Grande valley and many from settlements along the Pecos river, joined the caravan of settlers into the land of the buffalo and Comanche.

San Hilario, on the Canadian river, was founded by Don Hilario Gonzáles, who ran sheep on a thousand hills, as the old-timers used to say. Don Hilario was a very influential man in his day. Even half a century after he passed on, he was remembered and mentioned as the wealthiest man in the '70's. I knew his two daughters, Doña María Ignacia Baca and Doña Juanita Martinez. In about 1860 he built the San Hilario chapel to which the settlers from the Llano and the Ceja traveled many miles to hear Mass.

Every town which had a chapel, dedicated it to the patron saint of the founder. The scattered ranches did not have chapels, but a room in the home of a prominent rancher was set aside for worship and this also had a patron saint.

The plaza of San Lorenzo was about ten miles from San Hilario and five miles from the present Conchas Dam. Don

Francisco López, whose flocks and herds ran into the thousands, founded the town of San Lorenzo. Don Francisco came from Santa Fe. His son, Don Lorenzo, was one of the best-known and most respected citizens in the territory. The chapel, built by his father about 1860, had San Lorenzo as the patron saint. In 1880 there was a newspaper in San Lorenzo called *The Red River Chronicle,* which ran two editions, one in English and one in Spanish.

In 1824, Don Pablo Montoya from La Cienega, near Santa Fe, was given a land grant extending from the Ceja to the Río Colorado (the Canadian river). Don Pablo was instrumental in organizing the early Llano settlers and leading them against the nomadic Apaches and Navajos.

From the Montoya heirs a part of the Pablo Montoya Grant was purchased by Don Francisco López and Don Hilario Gonzáles.

Don Francisco had several beautiful daughters. Two of the Romero brothers from Las Vegas, Don Trinidad and Don Eugenio, married Valeria and Chonita. In 1890 Don Trinidad and Don Eugenio, who with Don Trinidad's son operated a large mercantile business in Las Vegas, sold their livestock holdings in San Miguel County to the Bell Ranch which also took over the Pablo Montoya Grant and other surrounding land. The deal consisted of twelve thousand head of cows, most of them with calves. Papá, who was a first cousin of the Romeros, helped with the rounding up and delivering of the cattle. It was a big event and one of the largest transactions of that era. The Romeros operated their business under the name of T. Romero Brothers and Son.

The Romero brothers also ran thirty thousand head of sheep at Ojo de la Mula near the Bell Ranch. Román, son of Don Trinidad, and who is now past eighty, related to me that one spring he had come home from a college in St. Louis to spend the Easter holidays. It was a very cold season with snow on the ground. His father sent him to Ojo de la Mula to help with the lambing. In order to save the lambs they had to keep fires burning around the flocks. It was quite an experience for a tenderfoot.

Don Trinidad Romero was delegate to Congress from New Mexico in 1877-79. In 1880 he built a $100,000 mansion at Romeroville, near Las Vegas, where he entertained many notables, among them President and Mrs. Hayes, General Sherman and General Grant.

Many of the smaller ranchers who lived between the Pecos river and Oldham County, Texas, came there through the influence of Don Hilario Gonzáles and Don Francisco López. Some of them were relatives, others *empleados* or friends of the families who took sheep and cattle on the shares from them.

A great number of the Hispanos who settled the Panhandle of Texas went there from San Hilario, San Lorenzo, Las Vegas, Mora and the Pecos River country. They were the first settlers of now-extinct plazas with sonorous Spanish names.

Don Agapito Sandoval and Don Casimiro Romero from Mora were the founders of Atascosa in Oldham County, Texas. Don Agapito left the Llano country in 1888 about the same time Don Casimiro moved to El Médano, about fifteen miles from the town of Endee and close to San Jon. At El Médano, Don Casimiro opened a store after the sheep business became impossible. One night after he had closed his store, he was assaulted by masked bandits, supposedly Texans, who robbed him of almost everything which he possessed in the mercantile business. When Don Casimiro moved to Atascosa, the buffalo were still grazing on the plains. Besides his sheep interests, he freighted goods to

70

and from Dodge City, Kansas. He remained in the Llano country until his death.

Don Mariano Montoya, who was the first county clerk of Oldham County, created in 1881, was still running sheep on the Texas side at the beginning of the twentieth century. He went to Atascosa in 1878. When the homesteaders came, it became harder and harder to find pastures for the sheep and Don Mariano moved to Logan, just inside the New Mexico line.

Arroyo de Trujillo joins the Canadian River at the point where the settlement named for the arroyo stood. A Frenchman ran a store there in the days of the sheepmen, but the *patrón* was Don Jesús María Trujillo. He had many *empleados* and they, with their families and the family of the *patrón,* made up most of the population.

Don Pablo Garcia y Apodaca was living in San Hilario in 1874. Like many others, he took cattle on the shares from Don Hilario Gonzáles and moved to the Plaza Larga country and lived at Ojo del Carnero. His daughter, Jesusita, married Antonio Chávez and they moved to Las Salinas on the Texas side. Las Salinas was an important plaza. Salinas means salt mines, and salt mining was an industry there. Men came from Antonchico, Puerto de Luna, Lincoln, Las Vegas and other points in New Mexico for their salt supplies. Some of the settlers along the Salinas made a living by going into Colorado and New Mexico to sell the salt.

Don Emeterio Gallegos was a merchant in Las Salinas. He moved to Logan when the Texans pushed the New Mexicans over the line.

In Rito Blanco lived Don José and Don Miguel Tafoya. They moved to the Clayton vicinity and some of their descendants are living there today.

Don Higinio Esquibel dwelt at Ojo del Llano. There were many families in this plaza, mostly the *empleados* of the Esquibel family. The chapel built there by Don Higinio in 1880 was dedicated to *El Santo Niño de Atocha,* the Holy Child. The Texas Hispanos came there to hear Mass. This part of the country is known as Revuelto, and it is east of Tucumcari just over the Texas line.

The San Rafael chapel, built in 1875 at Pajarito by Don Gregorio Flores, was the early gathering place of worship for families who lived on ranches between what is now Tucumcari and east to the Texas line, as well as those living as far west as Cuervo. It was six miles from the railroad station of Montoya on the Southern Pacific.

Don Apolinar Vigil was the *patrón* at Saladito. In 1880, a chapel was erected there and dedicated to *Nuestro Padre Jesús.* Associated with the chapel was a *morada* maintained by the Penitentes as a place of worship serving the Society's members over the Ceja and the Llano.

Nueve Millas was the home of Don Sabino and Don Pablo Martínez. In Los Alamitos, Don Lorenzo Otero and Don Filomeno Chávez had their sheep ranches and there also lived Don Pedro and Don Macario Chávez. These men had small herds of sheep, a thousand or two head.

ALL the ranchers had some cattle, but until late in the 1890's the Llano was primarily a sheep country.

My grandfather, Don Tomás D. Cabeza de Baca was running fifteen thousand head of sheep on the Plaza Larga country in 1875. In the Pajarito country, where Newkirk is now, he ran more than two thousand head of cattle. In those days there were no bonding companies. My grandfather was one of the bonds-

72

men of the newly-elected San Miguel County sheriff-clerk-treasurer, which offices were held by one man. At the end of his term, the officer was short in the county funds. Grandfather had to produce $40,000. Ewes were worth one dollar per head, cows seven dollars. He sold all his livestock and to make up the balance, he mortgaged 100,000 acres of his land grant, El Valle Grande in Sandoval county, to Don José Leandro Perea for $10,000.

After that time Grandfather managed to increase his flocks and herds to a few thousand, but he never became wealthy. Until his death, he was part owner of the 100,000 acres of the Baca Location Number Two (now part of the Bell Ranch), which later was paid to lawyers trying to save the other three Baca locations.

Don Cruz Gallegos, from Upper Las Vegas, stopped at our *rancho* on his way to oversee his sheep camps near Endee as late as 1913. At that date there still was a handful of Las Vegas sheepmen trying to hold their grazing land, but one by one they gave up as the homesteaders took up the land.

The Hispanos had almost no titles of ownership, and the few who did were not able to compete with the newcomers. The boundaries had been laid by means of indefinite markers and much of the land was lost even after it was taken up by the courts. The history of the New Mexican land grants would fill volumes, but it is not a part of this story.

Those who settled on the Ceja and the Llano, took it for granted that the land was theirs. No other civilized people had become interested in the country until the New Mexican pioneers had made it safe for colonization.

A few of the Hispanos who had taken advantage of the homestead law of 1862 by taking up 160 acres of land remained on the Ceja along the Pajarito country.

73

In 1900, Don Benigno Benavídez built a chapel on his ranch six miles west of Montoya. I went to Mass there occasionally on my visits to our *rancho*. The chapel was dedicated to Our Lady of Guadalupe. Don Benigno was one of the few men running sheep in the early 1900's. There was also Don Bruno Martínez who lived at Carrizito. After the homesteaders started to take up the land, both men turned to raising cattle.

La Manga, near the Mesa Rica and adjacent to what is now Conchas Dam, was an important settlement in the 1890's. The population was made up of relatives and *empleados* of Don Francisco López and Don Hilario Gonzáles, who moved over from San Hilario and San Lorenzo. A chapel dedicated to San Luis Gonzaga was built about 1890. Don Felipe and Don Juan Delgado, who married two of Don Francisco López' daughters, also lived at La Manga. Later Don Domingo Maes, Don Benito Encinias and Don Juan López were running cattle in the area; some of their descendants still hold the land and raise cattle. Don Isidoro Gallegos lived at the foot of the Mesa Rica and with his sons, had a good sized cattle ranch.

Don Pedro Romero, Don Luciano López, and the Vigil brothers—Don Francisco, Don Doroteo and Don Manuel—lived at El Valle about ten miles from the present Newkirk. Some of the López and Vigil families still hold a few thousand acres there.

My father, Don Graciano, lived at Carrizito and later moved to Pajarito close by. Some members of our family are still ranching in both areas.

In 1905, a chapel was built in Newkirk and dedicated to the Holy Family. This chapel now serves the few El Valle, Carrizito and Pajarito Hispano families.

74

CUERVO CREEK has its source at the edge of the Staked Plains, about five miles southwest of the village of Cuervo which derives its name from the creek. It was founded when the railroad came in. A chapel dedicated to St. Anne was built in 1903. This town has lasted because there are still sheep and cattle ranchers in its vicinity who have managed to survive because their lands were on the Spanish and Mexican land grants and not opened to the homesteaders. Cuervo Peak, five miles west of the creek and fifteen miles from the head of the arroyo, is a majestic butte, overlooking the Llano for many miles. This landmark guided the Conquistadores in their early explorations. The Coronado route lies just south, by the foot of the peak and north of the Varejón Ceja. It was the junction of trails to the buffalo country.

The Cuervo country was the grazing land for the sheep and cattle herds of the Rio Grande settlers as early as 1780 and it is still settled by a few of the descendants of the same Spanish families. The first ranch house, built in the vicinity of the present village of Cuervo, was that of Don Eduardo Martínez, who came from Antonchico in 1870. The ruins of the house can be seen a quarter of a mile south of U.S. Highway 66, three miles west of the village of Cuervo.

The chapel at the railroad station of Montoya, dedicated to Joan of Arc, replaced the San Rafael chapel after the coming of the railroad.

Las Colonias, on the Pecos River, was settled by people from Cebolleta and Cubero, in the Lower Rio Grande and one still finds families of pure Castilian extraction living in that town. The handsome chapel there is well preserved.

Santa Rosa, where Don Celso Baca reigned as sheep and cattle king, had a private chapel in 1868. The home on Don Celso's hacienda is one of the few landmarks still preserved, but the chapel is in ruins. Don Celso's mother was Doña Rosa, and he dedicated the chapel to her memory. The town took its name from the patron saint of the church. Until the coming of the railroad, this stretch of country was known as Agua Negra, the name of the Antonio Sandoval Land Grant.

When Don Celso Baca built the Santa Rosa chapel on his hacienda, an old painting of Santa Rosa de Lima, brought over the Chihuahua Trail, adorned the altar. In later years, when the transition came, replacing the old with the new, Don Celso purchased a modern statue of Santa Rosa and this is the one which today is in the church at Santa Rosa.

Before the American occupation and until 1857, San Miguel del Vado was the parish seat for all the country east and south of the Pecos river into Texas. The church in San Miguel del Vado was built about 1806 and the first resident priest, as far as I can determine, was Father José Francisco Leyba.

From family papers, I learned that the town of San Miguel was settled by Tlascalan Indians, the descendants of the Mexican Indian servants the Spaniards brought with them during the Reconquest in 1693. When these Indians became unruly in Santa Fe, the viceroy of Mexico appointed Don Luis María Cabeza de Baca, my great-grandfather, from La Peña Blanca, as overseer

to take them into other territory. San Miguel del Vado, on the banks of the Pecos river, was chosen as the site for colonizing and settling of these *genízaros*. Here, Don Luis María supervised the building of homes, cultivating of the land, construction of dams and the erection of a church.

In later years, after the death of Don Luis María, the *genízaros* emigrated to Antonchico, La Cuesta, Chaperito and other surrounding villages. Hispano colonizers, then, seeking farming lands, populated San Miguel del Vado.

WITH the exception of San Miguel del Vado, no other parish served so large a territory as did Antonchico prior to the founding of the Chaperito and Puerto de Luna parishes. Antonchico served all that is today Guadalupe, Quay, De Baca, parts of Lincoln, eastern and southern San Miguel, Union and Harding counties and scattered settlements all along the Llano including northwest Texas.

In 1857, Father John B. Fayet founded the Antonchico parish, and it was not until then that the people of the plains had access to a church east of the Pecos river.

Antonchico was settled in 1834 by a group of families who were given a tract of land, known as the Antonchico Grant. In the confirmation of the grant, the names of these families appear: Salvador Tapia, Bernardo Ulibarrí, Felipe Valencia, Luis Gonzales, Tomas Martín, Miguel Martín, José Medina, Simón Estrada, Lorenzo Tapia, Diego Antonio Tapia, Mariano Aragón, Francisco Baca, Rafael Durán, Juan Sebastian Durán, José Durán, and Juan Cristobal García. These settlers came from San Miguel del Vado and many of their descendants still live there.

Antonchico, originally named Sangre de Cristo, was a settlement of about six hundred inhabitants in 1842 when the expedition of good will led by General McCleod crossed the Llano on its way to Santa Fe, and about which I heard from Papá.

In 1841, an expedition left Austin, Texas, with the General in command of about thirty-two men as troops. Merchants accompanied the troops, because—according to history—the object of the operation was to establish commercial relations between Texas and New Mexico. The expedition was well armed with artillery.

The Texas Congress had approved a law appropriating all the territory east of the Rio Grande and members of the good will mission were hopeful that the New Mexicans were dissatisfied with their government and would be willing to become a part of Texas.

After suffering untold hardships, the men under General McCleod reached New Mexico, but the ruling element in Santa Fe already knew about the good will excursion on its way to this territory. The Texas men were met by General Armijo's army from Santa Fe at Laguna Colorada (Red Lake) at the mouth of Bull Canyon, just over the Ceja of the Llano. When the McCleod army reached the Staked Plains, they nearly perished from hunger and thirst. They stopped at the sheep camp of Don Tomás Francisco Cabeza de Baca at Laguna Colorada to secure food when they were overtaken by Armijo's army.

One of the sheepherders who was at the camp lived to a very old age and served my grandfather, Don Tomás Dolores Cabeza de Baca, a brother of Don Tomás Francisco. It was he who related to Papá about the McCleod men stopping there for assistance. In this sheep camp, the Texans traded a spring wagon to the herders for meat. General Armijo's men led the McCleod unorganized men into Antonchico and there arrested the vanguard which had preceded the expedition. It was well known that McCleod was seeking the annexation of New Mexico to Texas. Don Pablo Aragón, who later lived at Newkirk as our neighbor, used to relate that he was a boy about seven years old when the McCleod army was brought into Antonchico. He remembered that he and other boys climbed the corn cribs and brought down ears of corn for the hungry Texans.

I KNEW Puerto de Luna when it was a parish seat, with visitas as far away as Tucumcari. Puerto de Luna was founded by colonists from the lower Rio Grande in New Mexico in 1862; it was then a *visita* of Antonchico. The Puerto de Luna church was built in 1881, and became a *parroquia,* parish church, in 1896. Father Simon Alvernhe was the first pastor. In 1920, the parish seat was moved to Santa Rosa.

The first Mass celebrated in Puerto de Luna was for the funeral of Don Juan Patrón, who was murdered by a Texan, an emissary of the Murphy-Dolan faction which figured prominently in the Lincoln County War. It was through Don Juan's generosity that the church had been completed and fate had it that he enter it as corpse.

Before the coming of the railroad, Puerto de Luna was the county seat of Guadalupe County.

My baptismal certificate is in the Chaperito church, a *parroquia* which for more than half a century served hundreds of miles on the Llano. Chaperito became a parish in 1876, with Father Juan B. Galon as its first pastor. He served until 1884. Records show that the Chaperito church once had jurisdiction over all the Llano country. There are baptismal entries in the early 1880's from Atascosa, Trujillo, Ojo de San Juan, Las Salinas and Mobeetie in Texas, and from Revuelto, San Lorenzo, San Rafael and Cuervo, in New Mexico.

9. Las Vegas Grandes

SAN MIGUEL HAS BEEN CALLED THE "EMPIRE COUNTY" of New Mexico. It has an area of 4,749 square miles. Las Vegas, its largest town, has figured most prominently in its history.

In 1821, Don Luis María Cabeza de Baca from La Peña Blanca, petitioned the government for a tract of land in the names of himself and his seventeen male children. The land was called Las Vegas Grandes, and the boundaries as claimed were: On the north, the Sapello river; on the south, San Miguel del Vado; on the west, the Pecos mountain; on the east, El Aguaje de la Yegua and the Antonio Ortiz Grant.

In 1823, Don Luis María was given title to the land. He took possession of the land and lived there for a number of years. He had great dreams of an empire in the name of Cabeza de Baca, but the Indian raids from the north made it impossible for him to continue living on the land which consisted of half a million acres. At the time, he also had a large tract of land known as El Ojo del Espiritu Santo in what is now Sandoval County near his home at La Peña Blanca. The latter grant consisted of about 113,141 acres.

These facts I know from family tradition, for Don Luis María was my great grandfather, and I remember when my grandfather received some money from the sales of some of the land.

80

I was a very small child, but the name of Don Luis María, for whom my brother was named, was very important in our family. I heard many times that when he was living he held a very prominent part in the government of the province of New Mexico. It is told that when a new governor arrived in New Mexico, Don Luis mounted his mule, and with his bodyguard went to Santa Fe to greet the newcomer. If my great-grandfather liked him, all was well, but if he displeased Don Luis, soon a letter went to the Viceroy of Mexico to replace the governor—and he was replaced.

Don Luis María died in La Peña Blanca in 1833, but his heirs continued to hold to the Las Vegas Land Grant. With the coming of the Santa Fe Trail, Las Vegas began to be populated and soon became an important stop on the trail. The citizens of Las Vegas petitioned that they be given title to the grant, and after reaching an agreement with the heirs of Don Luis María, the land was turned over to the petitioners. In the agreement with the government, the Cabeza de Baca heirs were given five tracts of land known as the Baca locations, each consisting of approximately 100,000 acres. My grandfather inherited Baca Location Number One, known as El Valle Grande, near Los Alamos of atomic renown.

My grandfather, Don Tomás D. Cabeza de Baca, moved to Las Vegas from La Peña Blanca in 1865. He built his home on the east side of the Plaza and there conducted a mercantile business. He also owned wagons which freighted over the Santa Fe Trail. His sheep and cattle grazed on the Ceja.

From my grandparents, I learned much of the early history of Las Vegas. On the plaza lived Don Romualdo Baca, Don Miguel Desmarais, and Don Miguel Romero. The Catholic church was on the west side of the plaza, but in later years, Don Romualdo Baca gave a tract of land for building a new church, which still stands. My grandmother used to tell that when they excavated for the foundation of the new church, the priest asked that the bodies which had been buried in the church cemetery be moved to the new location. Those who had relatives claimed the bodies, and they were placed inside the foundation of the new structure. Don Romualdo, when donating the ground for the church, asked that he be buried inside the church, but when he passed away, another priest had jurisdiction and he was buried in the cemetery, although his family had a signed agreement concerning his burial.

In 1875, the Jesuit Fathers founded *La Revista Catolica,* a newspaper in Spanish, which had great circulation in the Southwest. In 1877, the same priests established the Jesuit College, which was a godsend to New Mexico and surrounding territory. Education had been possible only to those who could afford to send their children to Mexico, to the States or Europe. The priests were mostly Italians, but they must have been excellent teachers because my uncles and Papá, who received all their education there, had a wonderful command of the English language and a vast knowledge of the arts and sciences. My education seems meager compared to theirs.

Later the College was moved to Denver and is now Regis College. *La Revista Católica* remained in Las Vegas until 1918, when it was moved to El Paso, Texas, and still is published there.

The College was no longer in Las Vegas when I went there as a child, but the Jesuits had the newspaper and a chapel where I heard Mass. It was not the official parish, but the Las Vegas Catholics went there in larger numbers than to the parish church. The chapel was beautiful and I shall never forget the May devotions with the lovely Virgin, whose robes of satin were renewed each year. I still remember the beautiful hymns led by Father Alfonso Rossi, who had been professor of literature at the College. He was the director of the choir and he played the organ. One of my older cousins sang in the choir and I accompanied her to practice and to Mass on Sundays. In those days, a girl never went anywhere unless accompanied by her mother or a chaperone, and if an older person could not be on hand, a small child went along. It was my lot to be a companion to my older cousins, and often I was sworn to secrecy about them meeting their sweethearts on the way to church or other places.

I loved Father Rossi, he always had candy for me and refreshments for the girls in his choir. It was he who heard my first confession.

It was a sad day for Las Vegas when the Jesuits left. They had done much for the spiritual and educational needs of the people. I knew Father José Marra, who had been the Dean of the College and later director of the newspaper. He was a very learned man and he served as Superior of the Jesuit order.

The most saintly man I have ever known was Father Enrique Ferrari, who directed the printing of *La Revista Católica*. He came from the nobility of Italy and he was truly noble. From 1877 to 1880, he served as editor of the paper.

Two altar boys helped serve Mass on Sundays at the Jesuit chapel. As a small child, I remember Francisco Delgado and Pablo Hernandez as altar boys, and when Pablo left for Spain, my brother Luis and José Sena, a cousin, took their places.

When my grandfather was on his deathbed, he asked that one of the Jesuit priests hear his last confession. Although it was against the rules of the parish, Father Rossi came as a friend and confessor.

Las Vegas was the shopping center and market for the cattle

and sheepmen from the Llano country. It became the most important town of the territory. I remember we once considered Santa Fe and Albuquerque as mere villages.

The Sisters of Loretto came to Las Vegas in 1869. I went to their school in the grammar grades. Don Romualdo Baca gave the Sisters their home and three of his nieces joined the order. Girls from Las Vegas and all the surrounding country came to the day and boarding school. The daughters of the wealthy classes would never have been sent to a public school. Those who were poor often worked to earn their tuition, for it was a privilege to attend Loretto Academy. My mother received all her education from the Sisters in Las Vegas.

As I remember Las Vegas in my youth, it was a very democratic town. We lived on the Hot Springs Boulevard in Old Town. There were many beautiful homes in our neighborhood and nationalities were merged into one big family. There was no discrimination as to color or race. One of the best liked families was that of Montgomery Bell. He and his wife were mulattoes and I have never known finer persons. We had German, Jews, Spanish and plain American neighbors, but we all played together as one big family and we all loved the Bells. Mr. and Mrs. Bell were from the South; Montgomery Bell came with the Stephen Elkins family to New Mexico. He was the son of a slave of the Elkins. By thrift, he accumulated a large fortune and he was a friend of the poor people. He was their money lender.

As a child, I was a problem to my grandmother and was forever running away from her. She called me from morning till night trying to locate me. The Bells had a parrot and he learned to call me. Every Christmas Mr. Bell had a present for me from the Parrot. On one occasion he gave me a necklace with a small diamond from the parrot. I am sure that he did the same for all the neighborhood children.

One of the happiest recollections I have of Las Vegas concerns the Fourth of July celebrations. We always got new outfits for the occasion. By nine o'clock in the morning we were gathered on the plaza for the fiesta. The band played on the kiosk in the park all day. Around the park were stands selling ice cream, cold drinks, food and candies. In the afternoon there were races and the climbing of the greased pole and at night, they had fireworks. By nine o'clock the fiesta was over and we were a bunch of tired children full of ice cream and candy, for we had been saving money for the day ever since Christmas. It was the one day that there were no restrictions on the amount of money we spent nor a set hour for us to come home.

I do not remember when the Fourth of July celebration was discontinued, but after I was in my teens, the Cowboys' Reunion took its place. By then, there were too many outsiders and it was not as much fun. My experiences on the ranch did not make a rodeo interesting as I felt that it was not real.

I am sure Don Luis María never thought that the empire of which he dreamed would be the home of some of his descendants and that they would play an important part in its history. My grandfather was county commissioner during the litigation over whether the county seat should be in Old or New Las Vegas. He was instrumental in getting the vote for the old town and there the courthouse was built while he was in office. When the old courthouse was replaced during W.P.A. days, Las Vegas lost one of its most imposing structures. How well I remember, upon climbing the mesa on a return trip from our *rancho,* seeing the tower of the old courthouse and how happy it made me that our journey was ending and I would be in Las Vegas again.

My grandfather is buried in the church cemetery, but by the time grandmother died, a ban had been placed prohibiting burial there. She and her sons all lie in the Catholic cemetery, Monte Calvario, in Las Vegas Grandes, on the ground which had once been their land grant.

The cemetery lies in view of Hermit's Peak and it brings to my mind the story of the hermit which my grandmother enjoyed relating. A few years ago I was attending a 4-H club meeting in Las Gallinas at the foot of the Peak. The leader of the club was Mrs. Domitilo Martinez and she recognized me as one of the de Bacas who went camping in the Gallinas country many years before. I asked her if she knew any stories about the hermit, and to my surprise she had written the story as told by her father—who had known the hermit. She had written the story in Spanish and asked me if I would translate it for her. Many tourists come to her place and are always eager to hear the story. I did the translation, and in doing it I learned much that would have been lost of the personal side of the tale.

She relates that her grandfather was an adobe maker and had been hired by Don José A. Baca from Upper Las Vegas to do some work for him. He took one of his sons with him and Don José had liked the boy and he hired him as cowherder. One day, while he and other boys were herding the milk cows near Hot Springs, they saw a man walking along with a cane. He came towards them and asked them for a drink. They had no water and told him that they went to drink by the river which was quite a distance. It was a very hot day and they, too, were thirsty. The man told them: "You see those rocks there by the hillside, there is water there." The boys could not believe it as they knew the spot and they had never seen water there. They went to the place and there found a spring of clear water.

The man went on his way and finally reached Las Gallinas. The people were surprised to see a stranger, as in those days very few outsiders came to the village. Several of the villagers invited him to their homes, but he asked for a shed in which to put the things he had in a knapsack. In the evening he preached to the men and in a few days he had become part of the village. After a time, he asked the men to climb the Peak with him. No one had ever ventured the ascent, for the terrain was very craggy and rugged. He showed them the way and soon they were on top. There was no water anywhere and every few days some man went up to take him water. He started encouraging the men to come up to the Peak and there he fed them. He had some corn-meal from which he made gruel. Those who tasted it claimed that it was the most delicious food they had ever eaten, and the strange part of it was that they felt it was not going to be enough to fill them, yet after eating it, they felt satisfied.

One day, the hermit told them that they were going to find water. He led them to a rocky spot and with little effort water was found. The men were happy because the carrying of the water had been a difficult task.

He organized a society which he called the Society of the Holy Cross. They built a Via Crucis, and there they said the Stations of the Cross.

He lived alone on the Peak, but kept in contact with the villagers who lived below. Once in a while on Sundays, he came down and walked to Las Vegas and to hear Mass.

My grandmother used to relate that he was an Italian by the name of Juan Agostini and that he was friend of a relative of theirs who lived in Upper Las Vegas. He brought his clothing there for laundering and his undergarments were stained with blood, showing that he practiced penance. On the feast of the Holy Cross, which is the third of May, he built *luminarias,* little bonfires, on the peak and the people of Las Vegas would watch for them and joined in saying the rosary. When I was a child, he was long gone, but the Gallinas villagers kept up the practice and we joined in praying.

Mrs. Martinez did not seem to know of his departure from the Las Vegas country, but I heard the story from grandmother that he had decided to return to his native Italy. He travelled to Old Mesilla and there stayed with Father José de Jesús Cabeza de Baca, grandfather's brother, who was the resident priest at the time. The hermit went up in the Organ Mountains and there he lived in a cave. One day, he came down bringing his books and other possessions to Father de Baca. He told him that on the next day he was leaving for his journey into Mexico to take the boat and that evening he would light a bonfire and for him and his parishioners to join him in prayer. Father de Baca waited for the signal, but it never came. He waited several days and finally sent up to search for him. He was found murdered, supposedly with intent of robbery.

Mrs. Martinez, in her story, credits him with superhuman powers and tells of miracles performed, and that he could foretell events and even read peoples' minds. She claims that he was a priest, but I have not been able to confirm that fact.

The Gallinas residents at the foot of Hermit's Peak still practice the rites which Don Juan Agostini taught them.

IV. BAD MEN
& BOLD

10. Vicente Silva, Bandit Leader

WHILE I GATHERED MATERIAL FOR THIS BOOK, I made visits to men and women who were living in some of the San Miguel County communities at the time of Los Gorras Blancas. Among them was Don Luciano López, who is now past eighty and lives as our neighbor at El Valle.

In 1890, Don Luciano was living at La Concepción, about twenty miles east and south of Las Vegas. He tells that the citizens of the different communities who had sheep on the Ceja and Llano had banded together for protection against the building of fences on their grazing lands and to help each other with crops and farming in the communities. They called the organization Caballeros de Labor, Gentlemen of Labor.

The party served a good purpose, but as there is always some bad element in all organizations, politicians saw where they could gain prestige. In place of protection, this element wanted common pastures and since the cutting of fences on public domain had appealed to them, they carried the practice to the farming lands of the communities. These men called themselves El Partido del Pueblo, the People's Party. It became a secret society. They sent anonymous letters to those not in their party, threatening their lives and telling them that their fences would be cut down, their homes and farm buildings set on fire. They carried out their threats. Don Luciano tells how they tore down his father's gristmill and burned his barns and corrals. I remember my grandmother telling us about their fences being cut down at La Liendre. She heard the bandits when they came and she wanted to go out and fight, but Grandfather knew it would be suicide. Next morning miles and miles of their pasture and farmland fences were cut into fragments.

The respectable citizens could not go out at night without a bodyguard and heavily armed. They did not know who the members of the gang were—in many cases they were the same neighbors who had been Los Caballeros de Labor, as it was learned later.

These marauders wore white hoods over their heads when they were out pillaging and came to be known as Los Gorras Blancas, the White Caps.

For protection, the good citizens formed a new party which they called El Partido de la Unión, the Union Party, composed of members of both major political parties. They held community meetings and for protection they used a password in order to keep out those from the bad element who might seek admittance. Don Luciano served as secretary to El Partido de la Unión in 1891. He tells that there were men whom they never suspected as belonging to El Partido del Pueblo in the new organization and they served as spies for the corrupt politicians. The wife of one of these men once confided to a neighbor about her husband's work. She was found out and was given fifty lashes as punishment.

El Partido de la Unión became strong, but in it were many from the other faction. Often they would get rid of the good

90

citizens by breaking up the meetings with the pretense that it was late and proceed to their own haunts to plan their maraudings.

During this time the Republican Party was down. When it was built up again many who had been Republicans left El Partido de la Unión and joined the Democratic Party.

In going over grandfather's papers, I found a printed notice which explains El Partido de la Union, and which I have translated:

"BE ON THE WATCH
UNION PARTY OF SAN MIGUEL COUNTY!

"Being that a few days ago we have seen some leaflets signed by —————, as president of the Central Committee of the Union party, in which a call is made to the *Republican Unionists,* that they gather in convention on March 17, 1896 with the aim of dissolving the Union which now exists in our county; we wish to make public that said call is without the authority of the Central Committee of said party, which has neither been consulted nor has any Republican Unionist, being merely a wicked treason by means of which the president of the Central Committee of the Union Party desires to seek personal vengeance and for which end he wishes to use the people, who in our concept are not ready to lend themselves as instruments to satisfy personal vengeances for any person whoever he may be.

"Now, since it might happen that the Republican Unionists, who read the communication from said Señor —————, believe that the Union has dissolved and that the adherents of that party will have to follow whatever path they desire, we advise the people in general and our friends in particular that what the *President* exposes is only a trap built by others and signed by him

91

with the aim of breaking up the Union Party, which has been of great service and to form, not a political party, which they boast as the Republican party, but the old Ring so that they may divide among themselves the political offices and to bring to the people displeasure, rivalry, enmity, quarrels and general misery as were prevalent during the rule of some of the officials of a past administration, whose records form a black page in the history of our county.

"Wherefore, those of us who are signed publish the present notice to inform the people in general and to the loyal adherents of the Union Party that today, more than ever, we are ready to remain with the party which we formed of our own free will and with the will of the people, not with the aim of renouncing our political affiliations, but in order to hold back the reins of government from the hands of those who defalcated it, the protectors of all evil and political usurpers and in order to place it in the hands of honest and upright men.

"The reasons which motivated this declaration from us are here exposed and in conclusion we appeal to the patriotism of all the San Miguel County citizens to cooperate with us in upholding the Union Party which has to this day given us endearing results and thereby establishing, as everyone knows, peace and harmony in our county.

Very respectfully,"

There are forty-nine signatures to this paper, among them those of two of my uncles and many of our relatives and friends from both major political parties.

From the Gorras Blancas grew up another menace to the citizens of San Miguel and the surrounding counties and that was Vicente Silva and his forty bandits.

THE story of Vicente Silva made a very vivid impression on my early life. The crimes were committed by his gang before I was born, but I well remember hearing that on the day my brother Luis María was born, a messenger was sent to Las Vegas to notify our maternal grandfather, Don Cirilo Delgado, about the birth of his first grandchild. The messenger was Don Juan Aragón. The date was May 26, 1893. As he was riding along, he noticed a team of burros dragging something. He became curious and led his horse towards them and his words were: "Upon seeing such a horrible spectacle, my hair stood on end." The burros were dragging the bodies of two men who had been murdered by the Silva gang near El Vegoso, six miles east of Las Vegas. Again and again I heard the story and my hair also stood on end. Don Manuel Cabeza de Baca tells about the murder and I quote:

"On the 26th day of May, 1893, the people of Las Vegas were

greatly disturbed. Great excitement and consternation ruled the town upon hearing that two men had been murdered. Benigno Martinez was a sheep grower, who at great sacrifice had been able to accumulate about two thousand head of sheep, which he and his ill-fated companion were herding, unaware of danger when the black hand of Cecilio Lucero, a member of Silva's gang, came to exterminate them.

"Cecilio Lucero, cousin of Benigno Martinez, was married and with his wife lived in Benigno's house, where he was provided with all the considerations and favors of a friend and relative.

"The day before, Cecilio had been in Watrous, where he offered a bunch of sheep for sale—it is not known whether anyone accepted the trade or not. The following day, he went to the sheep camp of his cousin Benigno and there spent the night with him. At daybreak, without reason, he shot Benigno, killing him instantly and then turned and killed Juan Gallegos, who also died immediately. Not content with the bullets which pierced their bodies, he took a rock and smashed their heads; the victims remained unrecognizable except for their clothing and letters which they carried in their pockets and which were found when the investigation was conducted.

"To add to the crime, he tied a rope to a burro's neck and to the other end, he tied Benigno's feet; he did the same with the other victim.

"The asses dragged the bodies all day and all night, until next day when a man by the name of Juan Aragón, who was coming along the road, noticed the burros dragging something. Immediately he sped his horse and took the news into Las Vegas.

"In a short while the officers accompanied by a number of respectable citizens reached the scene of the crime.

94

"The excitement was general and hundreds of persons viewed the bodies and upon seeing them, they called for vengeance.

"It did not take long to find out who the murderer was. Cecilio Lucero was arrested and in the preliminary investigation, it was proved that he was guilty of the murder of Martinez and Gallegos. About three hundred persons gathered and at eleven o'clock that night they took Lucero out of jail and lynched him on a telephone post."

This was one of the early stories which I remember hearing. We moved to Las Vegas from my grandfather's hacienda of La Liendre in 1901. We lived in the home of my uncle, Don Manuel Cabeza de Baca, who wrote the Silva story. It was a spacious home built around a courtyard. We occupied the south wing of the house, and in summer evenings we sat out in the patio listening to stories and tales of perilous days in San Miguel County. It was in this same patio that, during the Silva terror, Uncle Manuel almost met his death. He and my Uncle Ezequiel, who later became Governor of New Mexico, were on Silva's blacklist. One night, as Uncle Manuel was leaving for an evening meeting, two masked men jumped from behind some lilac bushes. Don Manuel always carried a gun, but as he went to reach for it, the bandits fled. Later on, rumor spread that they had fled because a beautiful lady in white robes was accompanying him. No one was with him.

Uncle Manuel was a handsome man. He was not as tall as his brothers (Papá was six feet tall). He had deep blue eyes and the fairest skin I have ever seen. He dressed meticulously, always. He wore white stiff bosom shirts and a diamond stud under his black bow tie. His suits were grey or black and strictly tailored. On his right hand he wore a diamond ring which was most becoming to his soft white skin. He always carried a cane with a gold head and for special occasions, he dressed in his Prince Albert and stovepipe hat. I remember him well in that garb at my grandmother's funeral in 1912.

He was the oldest of six sons, and as was the custom in Spanish families, his brothers respected him completely. He received his early education at St. Michael's College in Santa Fe and at the Jesuit College in Las Vegas. Later he studied law under his friend, Ralph Emerson Twitchell, and was admitted to the bar in 1880. In 1886, he served as a member of the House in the territorial legislature from San Miguel County and was voted Speaker of the House for that term. In 1899-1901, he was Superintendent of Public Instruction, and in 1904, he again went as representative from Guadalupe County, then Leonard Wood County. He was a stanch Republican, but in 1912 he voted for his brother, who ran for Lieutenant Governor on the Democratic ticket in the first state election.

Besides his law practice, he engaged in cattle raising on the Ceja with Papá. It was he who hired El Cuate as ranch cook.

He was a very proud man, but after his death, we found out that he was quite a humanitarian. His books were filled with cancelled debts of poor people who were unable to pay him for his services as a lawyer. From the time of the coming of the railroad into Las Vegas and until his death, he was lawyer for the Atchison, Topeka and Santa Fe.

In 1896, Don Manuel Cabeza de Baca wrote the story of Vicente Silva and his bandits. It was published by *La Voz del Pueblo,* a newspaper printing office owned by Don Felix Martínez, Don Antonio Lucero and Don Ezequiel Cabeza de Baca in Las Vegas. In its day, *La Voz del Pueblo* was the most influential New Mexican newspaper printed in Spanish. It was a paper leaning decidedly toward the Democratic party.

At the turn of the century, the Vicente Silva story was still vivid in the experience of the Las Vegas inhabitants. I remember passing the Buffalo Saloon on the plaza and seeing some of the characters who still remained of what had been the Silva henchmen. Some had served their sentences, others had been pardoned for having given information about the crimes committed. I knew Julian Trujillo, who drove a coal wagon for many years. El Moro, El Lechuza and El Cachumeno were those who hung around the Buffalo Saloon and the ones who impressed me. As I recall, they looked the part of criminals or perhaps they appeared so to my imagination. They were poorly dressed and they carried a sad look on their faces. I was afraid to meet them, but that was only childish fear.

Although my uncle relates that Jose Chávez y Chávez was sentenced to be hanged, in 1920 my brother Luis met him in Pintada at a political rally. He was very old and blind.

El Cachumeno was herding sheep for one of my brothers-in-law near Las Vegas in 1929. He was very old then. He was a short man and quite bent from age.

Before I was ten years of age, I had read the Silva story written by my uncle—but it was only a review, for I knew every story by tradition. I knew every landmark relating to the items in the story and often I rambled around the terrain.

Don Manuel describes Vicente Silva thus:

"Vicente Silva was born in Bernalillo County, Territory of New Mexico, of poor but respectable parents in the year 1845. He never attended school and was, therefore, illiterate. On first appearance he gave the impression of being an honorable man. He was tall and well-built, and his personality helped to hide his inner self.

"Those who knew him well, liked him and one never

97

dreamed that such a human had been born to lead a life of crime and that in that handsome body dwelt the most perverse soul. It seems that the Devil had endowed him with all that is vile and corrupt.

"Vicente Silva had lived in Las Vegas for more than fifteen years. Soon after his arrival there, he opened a saloon and gambling house where by 1892 he had a large clientele made up of men and women whom the law brands as outcasts. The saloon was open at all hours and it never lacked wine, women and song.

"Among the notorious women who frequented Silva's place of drink were: One called La Golondrina, the Swallow, and two nicknamed Las Elefantas, the Elephants.

"Silva's house of drink and gambling, was a two-story structure; besides the rooms used for selling liquor and gambling, there were many others where Silva and his accomplices held their crime conferences.

"Silva was married, and his immediate family was composed of his wife, Doña Telesfora Sandoval, her brother, Gabriel Sandoval, and an adopted daughter, whose origin and birth will hold an important part in this story."

Often when I was in church or at a celebration where many people gathered, I wondered if Emma Silva was one of the persons around me. I heard the story about her adoption many times. The infant had been found in a stable run by John Miner. I always heard that she was a beautiful child and perhaps of Nordic extraction. It was only by eavesdropping that I heard the story. Our family did not discuss subjects pertaining to morality in the presence of minors, but we managed to run errands when our grandmother and her guests were conversing and in this way we learned the facts of life and the current gossip—mostly in small doses, but enough to arouse our curiosity. Vicente Silva and

98

his wife Doña Telesfora, were childless, and when the child came up for adoption they were given the preference, and she became Emma Silva. It was said that both Silva and his wife as well as Doña Telesfora's brother, Gabriel, loved the child very much. The sad part of it was that Silva, in order to show off the child, took her to the saloon, yet she had the protection of her foster mother who brought her up with the most patient and moral care that was possible in their surroundings.

Doña Telesfora knew of Silva's shady enterprises, yet she never dreamed that he would harm their adopted daughter. When the girl was old enough to go to school, she was placed in Loretto Academy, where the daughters of the most respectable families in Las Vegas and surrounding territory received their education.

On the morning of January 23, 1893, Emma was sent to school as usual. By noon she always came home for her midday meal. She did not come at the usual time and Doña Telesfora became alarmed. She walked to the Academy and, on the way, she was informed by one of the students that at ten o'clock that morning Emma had climbed into a carriage. Doña Telesfora sounded the alarm of the disappearance. Several days passed and she had had no word of her child. Both she and her brother were grief-stricken.

By this time Silva was becoming obsessed with the idea that his wife and brother-in-law were planning to expose him. He hated them and wished to do something to punish them. His first act was to call a meeting of two of his accomplices, one called El Mellado, Toothless, and the other El Lechuza, the Owl. He told them that Gabriel Sandoval, his brother-in-law, was their enemy and they must get rid of him. Their rendezvous was in

Los Alamos, a village twelve miles northeast of Las Vegas. As soon as their plans for the murder of Gabriel were completed, Silva sent El Lechuza, the most cunning of his companions in crime, to Las Vegas to look over the situation in Doña Telesfora's house. He found that they had guests, so the murder was postponed until the next night.

Silva had a paramour who was his confidant. He went to her home that evening and revealed to her his plans for killing his brother-in-law. The woman, whom Don Manuel called Flor de la Peña, was frightened at the thought of murdering a man whom she considered innocent of attempted betrayal. Flor knew than Doña Telesfora was jealous of her, but felt that she had a right to be, for Silva and Flor had been indiscreet. She was with child by Silva and she begged him not to commit the intended crime. Silva would not listen to her. Flor knew there was nothing she could do but keep quiet.

Besides the services of El Mellado and El Lechuza, Silva had secured the help of three of the city policemen, Chávez y Chávez, Julian Trujillo and a man named Alarid. They were part of his gang, yet no one suspected them as other than honorable law enforcement officers.

The kidnapping of Emma had a great effect on Gabriel Sandoval, and Silva knew well that he would leave no stone unturned until she was found. With the pretense that he knew the whereabouts of Emma, Julian Trujillo lured Gabriel into the trap. He told him that he was taking him to Flor de la Peña's home where Silva was hiding Emma. He also told him that they would have the help of the other two policemen. At eight o'clock that evening, they would meet at the appointed place.

By this time it was known that the abductor of Emma had been El Lechuza. As Gabriel was leaving Trujillo, he met the abductor and was about to strike him, but Trujillo intervened. El Lechuza denied any connection with or knowledge of Emma's disappearance. He then proceeded to de la Peña's home to inform Silva that all was in order for Gabriel's murder.

Gabriel had been asked not to relate anything to his sister about the plan to take Emma from Silva, but he was so happy over his success that he told her all. She promised to wait patiently, and he left full of hope. In front of the Buffalo Saloon he met the policemen; they turned towards the Catholic church on their way to Flor's house. Silva was waiting by the ruins of the old Alcalde house. As they approached, he jumped from behind the walls while Alarid and Chávez held Sandoval. Gabriel then knew that he had been betrayed.

Silva had a dagger in his hand. Gabriel begged for mercy, but Silva had none. The two policemen fired on him and Silva thrust the dagger into Sandoval's heart. Silva and El Lechuza dragged Sandoval toward Moreno Street until they reached an old house directly back of Silva's saloon. They threw the body into a hole which had served as a latrine for the saloon. They covered the body with dirt and trash. Doña Telesfora waited for her brother, but when morning came and he had not returned, she went to Uncle Manuel's office. She related to him the incidents leading to her brother's absence. Don Manuel proceeded to the office of the Police Judge. Here I quote from my uncle's relation of the interview:

"Knowing Silva's reputation, immediate action had to be taken to find out if Sandoval had met with foul play.

"Señora de Silva received encouragement and left with great hopes that soon she would hear from her brother.

"About six o'clock that evening of February 14th, one day after Sandoval's disappearance, the author of this story stepped into the office of the Police Judge, who then was Capt. José L. Galindre, a fearless man.

" 'What brings you, Señor de Baca?' he asked.

" 'I need the Chief of Police to help find a young man who has disappeared!'

" 'That is serious,' he said, 'Quite often persons come here to report lost women, but men—'

" 'The loss of a man is more serious than that of a woman.'

" 'There is a little egotism in your reply,' said the judge.

" 'I shall explain: A woman may be lost because her lover has kidnapped her and her disappearance which may cause her family grief, may cause her joy. When a man disappears he may be in a hospital, a suicide, or in jail, or—'

" 'And do you fear that the man you seek may have met with foul play?'

" 'I am afraid so; he has not been home since nine o'clock last evening. I can assure you that Sandoval, if he were alive, would not have failed to come home to his sister's home to sleep or to eat his meals because he has always been punctual, and therefore, I fear that something has happened to him.'

"The Police Judge left his office and in a few minutes he was back and said he had sent for the police chief who in effect came in a brief while.

" 'What do you wish, Señor Galindre?' he asked.

" 'Mr. de Baca wishes to know the whereabouts of Gabriel Sandoval who has disappeared and I ask you to leave no stone unturned until you find him.'

"He answered, 'All the police force is in charge, for I had already been notified about this disappearance. I have conducted some investigations and I believe he has left town.'

"Mr. de Baca said, 'Knowing his habits, I know he would not

102

have left without informing his sister, so I fear that he has met with some mishap.'

'Anyway,' said the police judge, 'it is urgent that you bring all your forces together with your bloodhounds and search every corner for the missing man.'

'I shall do so,' said the Chief of Police, and he departed.

"He went towards police headquarters and once there, he called Julian Trujillo, Chávez and Alarid, and told them what he had learned from the police judge. They, of course, promised to start the search at once, and they did. They looked everywhere except in the vile hole in which they had buried him. Finally they reported that they could find no clues except that someone had said that at El Puertecito (now Romeroville), a man had been hanged on a pine tree and it might be Sandoval.

"Doña Telesfora, knowing that Julian Trujillo was to have been with her brother the night before, went to inquire from him, as he had promised to help Gabriel bring Emma back. Trujillo denied everything but promised to help in the search in every way possible. They went to El Puertecito and searched every possible place but found no one hanged as had been reported. They returned satisfied that the rumors of a man having been hanged there were without foundation. Gabriel's disappearance remained a deep mystery."

THE old bridge dividing the towns of East and West Las Vegas is one that I shall never forget. It was one of those huge structures of steel which today have disappeared in most places. The old bridge had a history behind it which made it a landmark. Some of our shopping was done in New Town, as we called East Las Vegas. We lived in Old Town. The Gallinas river divides the two towns, and it was the old bridge we had to cross when I

103

was a child. Every time we crossed, I lived the stories I had heard about murders and criminals hiding under the bridge.

No story stood more vividly in my mind than the murder of Patricio Maes by the Silva bandits. Patricio was one of Silva's confederates. I do not know if it always rained or snowed when crimes were committed, but it seems that all storytellers in my young days made it quite dramatic by describing the weather. Be that as it may, one very cold and snowy night, while Las Vegas citizens slept, Silva and his gang were in conference planning the murder of one Patricio Maes.

For some reason or other, Silva suspected Patricio of betrayal. In the conference, he told his companions that they must do away with Patricio. They held a council among them similar to a court trial. Each member held a position in the court, and the trial continued to a late hour in the night. Most of the men were in favor of giving Patricio a chance; even as criminals, they must have felt that whatever Silva had against Maes, he had been one of them. The defendant was invited to the trial and he denied all the accusations. In those days the politicians in San Miguel county were divided into factions rather than parties.

I have told about the Gentlemen of Labor in another chapter. It seems that Maes had affiliated himself with this faction and it was the one waging war on the evildoers. The first offense of which Silva had been accused was the theft of some horses from Don Refugio Esquibel. Silva suspected Patricio as the informer. Whether Patricio was guilty of treason will never be known, but he was sentenced to die and on the appointed night he was taken to the bridge by the bandits. A rope was tied around his neck, one end was tied to one of the iron railings of the bridge. After he was dead, one of the men pushed the body into the air. As he did so, the noose gave way and Patricio fell into the river,

104

which in those days had water and this night was ice. They pulled the body back and left it hanging by the bridge. Next morning, Silva himself gave the alarm that a body was hanging by the river bridge. The police, who were Silva's accomplices, certainly were no help.

Another story which made the bridge memorable to me was about a man by the name of Carpio Saiz. This poor man had been the treasurer of the Sabinoso school on the Rio Colorado. He had come to Las Vegas to receive some money, $160, which had been apportioned to his school district. He was held up by the bandits as he crossed the bridge, and was murdered in cold blood under the bridge. His body was never found, but in those days many persons disappeared and were never found.

The old bridge was replaced by a concrete structure in 1909. This is the bridge which I crossed every day while I was attending high school and later college at what is today Highlands University. With the old bridge went all the memories, but it had to be that way, for Las Vegas became a different place from the one in which my uncles lived in terror.

In 1929, I was appointed Home Demonstration Agent for Santa Fe County. One of the scenic places which I visited once a month was the San Pedro country on the way to Cedar Grove. Many times as I drove through those piñons and junipers, I thought of this as Silva's paradise. And it is a paradise. This is the place which Vicente Silva selected to hide his loot. His manager was El Romo, Flat Nose, who took care of the horses, sheep and cattle which were taken from the San Miguel, Guadalupe and Mora county people. It was in this place that Don Refugio Esquibel found his horses branded with Silva's mark and which proved his first offense. After that he had to go in hiding, but the crimes continued.

105

THE Silva terror did not die out for many years, at least not in the memory of the people. I must have been fourteen years of age one summer I spent with a cousin of mine who lived in Los Alamos. This village had been the hideout of Silva and his bandits. That summer I heard many stories about the pillaging and murders. One was the robbery of Mr. William Frank's store. At the time that I was there, Mr. Frank was still running his place of business. He was quite reticent and even though I tried to get the story from him, he did not tell much. Enough to arouse my curiosity. My cousin's father-in-law enjoyed telling stories, and from him I gathered a few details. The condition of the weather was always important.

On a rainy April night, Silva and his accomplices decided not to leave out Mr. Frank from their number of victims. In order to find out where the merchant kept his money, Silva sent one of his men by the name of Medrán to buy some liquor. He gave him a twenty dollar gold piece so that Mr. Frank would have to make change. Mr. Frank was not one to distrust his customers, and without any suspicion he went to his safe and got the change and gave it to Medrán. Medrán watched carefully and to his way of figuring, it appeared that there must have been three hundred dollars in the safe. This he reported to Silva.

They waited for Mr. Frank to retire, and to make sure that the villagers were not venturing out in the torrential rain. They put on their masks and then proceeded to the store which they entered by breaking the front door. The safe was a large one, weighing about a ton. In some way, the six men assigned to the robbery, who were El Mellado (Toothless), El Moro (the Moor), El Patas de Mico (Monkey Feet), Dionicio Sisneros, Medrán, and Silva carried the safe to a wagon which they had left outdoors waiting. One saddled horse pulled the wagon.

106

They were not satisfied by taking the safe, which to their chagrin contained only forty dollars, but they took the books in which Mr. Frank kept his records of debts and other important papers which he kept in the safe. They built a fire and burned everything—papers only of value to Mr. Frank. Silva said to his companions, "Let us be charitable to the poor fools who owe money to the rich merchant." It was said that Mr. Frank lost over ten thousand dollars in debts, and possibly more.

Another story common in Los Alamos and which I heard during my visit there, was about the murder of Pedro Romero. This young man lived in Los Alamos. He fell in love with a

woman who had been married to Germán Maestas, a man who, when he was not in jail, had just been released from there. He had been one of Silva's henchmen. His marriage to the woman involved had not been announced or even registered. The woman, whose name was Rosa, took advantage of German's absence during one of his trips to the jail for some robbery which he had committed. She went after Romero and since she was an attractive woman, he married her. The ceremony was performed by El Mellado, who was then Justice of the Peace.

Germán heard about the marriage while he was in jail and he swore he would get revenge. He did not wait to finish his sentence. He was a trusty of the jailer, who was so accustomed to having him as a guest that he did not bother to watch him. With a companion he picked up, and a couple of horses which he roped in someone's pasture, he proceeded to Los Alamos. They found Rosa with Romero. After insulting him and beating him up, Germán took Rosa back to her home, which was about twenty miles distant. She did not remain there long; as soon as Germán had gone on one of his horse-stealing trips, she walked back to Los Alamos and joined Pedro, who had been left tied to a chair.

Germán was enraged with Rosa. That same day, he went in search of Jesús Vialpando, one of Silva's men, and in his company started a search for Rosa. Before arriving at Los Alamos, they spied a sheep camp. Being hungry they decided to stop and get breakfast. They had spent the night in search and had not had any food. Arriving at the camp, the dogs came after them. Maestas shot at them. The yelping of the wounded dogs reached the camp tent and who should come out but Pedro Romero, who was the overseer of the sheep. One can imagine his terror at seeing Maestas and Vialpando. They ordered him to prepare breakfast, which he did. Once the meal was over Maestas began insulting Romero. Romero had a gun, but before he could reach for it, Maestas and Vialpando fired and Romero fell dead into the embers of the fire he had built for the preparation of the meal. A small boy, who served as sheepherder, was the only witness of the crime. Maestas proposed to kill him, but Vialpando opposed it.

Soon after the bandits were out of sight, the thirteen-year-old boy removed Romero's body from the fire and started for Los Alamos to report the murder.

WRITING about Vialpando brings to mind another murder in which he was implicated. He and two other companions were on their way to San Pedro, in Santa Fe County, to sell some horses which they had stolen. After remaining a few days there, they were returning to Las Vegas. They stopped at the ranch of a man by the name of Tomás Martínez. There they killed a cow belonging to Martínez. About the time that they were cooking some of the meat, Tomás arrived on the scene. The bandits knew that the animal was one of his herd. Immediately, they planned to murder him. Tomás was accompanied by his dog. He reached the fire which the bandits had built and talking to them, he drew near to warm himself. The winter had been snowy and there was about eighteen inches of snow on the ground.

He noticed the cowhide near by, and as it was customary for cattle owners, he proceeded to examine it. While his back was turned, Vialpando fired two shots which killed Martinez. He and his companions took the body and placed it on the fire, adding more wood to make sure of its burning completely. One of them fired at the dog. The dog ran towards the house where Martinez lived, which was about six miles away. The Martinez family at first did not pay any attention to the dog; they thought Tomás would come along presently. The dog kept barking and howling, and finally aroused the family to suspect that all was not well. Some of the members started out, guided by the dog until they reached the place where the fire had burned. There was nothing but ashes and their thought was that Tomás might be frozen somewhere, and the dog was trying to tell them. The dog would not leave the spot. Finally one of the men noticed that the dog was digging in the ashes and succeeded in finding one of Tomás' legs which still had the shoe on. They scattered the ashes and there found the bones of their kinsman.

The ranch where the murder took place is on what is now called Glorieta Mesa, not far from the railroad station of Rowe, in San Miguel County. Feliciano Chávez had been Vialpando's partner in crime. My uncle, Daniel Cabeza de Baca, was Deputy Sheriff under his cousin, Don Hilario Romero, at the time, and it was they who arrested Vialpando and Chávez at Los Valles de San Agustín, near La Liendre.

The Martínez family were prominent citizens of Santa Fe County and my home in Santa Fe is built on the land which was originally theirs. I have heard the story from them on different occasions.

11. The Field
of Burdocks

FOR THREE YEARS, SAN MIGUEL COUNTY LIVED IN FEAR. Not a day passed when the citizens could have respite from the many crimes committed. It might be robbery, arson, rape or murder. A man by the name of Abraham Aboulafia, who had come from Turkey and who had a small business, was murdered and no one ever knew who killed him. He was the first victim found. After that, it was a daily occurrence. The purpose was robbery. Later the body of a tailor by the name of Jacob Stutzman was found in one of the arroyos near Las Vegas. His murder came out in the confession of the Silva bandits at their trial.

Vicente Silva became a fiend. Shortly after the murder of his brother-in-law, he sent a letter to his wife signed by her brother asking her to come to Los Alamos to join the brother, Silva and Emma. Doña Telesfora, who loved Silva, thought that perhaps he had repented and immediately made preparations for her departure. El Cachumeno, the Twisted One, was sent to take her to Los Alamos and with him he had a letter from Silva. I quote from the de Baca version:

"My dear Doña Telesfora:

"I hope this finds you in good health. Gabriel, Emma and I are well, thanks to God.

"The bearer of this letter has taken a wagon and he has his orders to bring all your furniture and other belongings, and he will take them to El Coyote where we shall establish our residence.

"I hope you will comply with my request to send your household things and tonight El Cachumeno will call for you. I shall meet you at Cañada Pastosa and as soon as we reach Los Alamos, I shall see that you join Emma and Gabriel.

"Make sure that your departure from Las Vegas will be as secret as possible. Wishing to see you, and with all my love,

Vicente Silva"

Doña Telesfora was extremely happy and she made plans for her husband's conversion into a respectable citizen. By nightfall, she had everything ready. She left for Los Alamos by an unfrequented road. At Cañada Pastosa she was met by Silva and El Lechuza.

In Los Alamos, five of his men were waiting for them. These were his best henchmen and for some time they had been dissatisfied with the way Silva was treating them. He gave them part of the loot, but they felt that they should have had more of it. On this night, they were known to be plotting against him. They had helped Silva to amass a fortune, and this time they planned to bring him to a compromise or else. Don Manuel Cabeza de Baca tells of the conversation in these words:

"One of the members of the gang who possessed more courage, spoke to them saying,

"'Let us be frank with one another; between friends there is no need to deny that while we remain under Silva's domination, we cannot get very far; we are in constant danger of falling into the hands of the law, and it is time that we sever our relations with him and divide the money which he has in keeping among our group. Tonight he will join his wife into eternity. He has gotten us into all these crimes and we have had enough. It is time that he pay his debts to Lucifer!

"'You are right,' answered all in one voice. 'Let us end it all tonight.'

"'If Silva kills his wife, I swear that I will get rid of him when he least expects it,' said one of the bandits, an obese man, frog-legged and one who was capable of disposing of Silva.

"The bandits agreed on their scheme and only awaited the proper moment.

"A few hours later after the men had made their plans, Silva arrived with his wife whom he had met at the appointed place. He sent El Lechuza back to Las Vegas to observe the reaction which Doña Telesfora's departure had upon the town's citizens."

SILVA arrived in Los Alamos with his wife on the night of May 19, 1893. He took her to the house where his henchmen were waiting. He ordered them to leave as he wanted to be alone with her.

As soon as they were alone he began to tell her that he must get away from the Las Vegas country and that he planned to take her to Taos with Gabriel and Emma who were now in El Coyote, near Mora.

The author of the Vicente Silva story who helped in getting

113

the confession at the trial of the bandits describes the scene as related to him by those who overheard it:

"'I have arranged in Fernando de Taos to establish our home there. In a few days you and the family will start for that place; I shall go to Las Vegas and settle some business that I have there, then I will join you.

"'I wish you would let me have whatever money you may have with you in case I should need it, because the little money I had, I left in Taos to be delivered to you upon arrival there.'

"Doña Telesfora thought it strange that Silva would want to take her money and at first she refused to part with it, but finally turned over two hundred dollars to him. After taking the money, Silva said, 'I would now like to have your jewels.'

"Doña Telesfora, who was an intelligent woman, immediately sensed that something was amiss. 'Why would you want my jewels?' she asked. 'Perhaps to give them to your paramour.'

"Silva, at the mention of his mistress became furious and angrily said, 'Do not dare talk like that. Seal your wretched lips.'

"'The truth hurts you, does it not?'

"'It is true that I love Flor more than I do you.'

"'Then you are not only a criminal but a despicable person.'

"'And you accuse me of being a criminal, you the only being on earth who might overlook it?'

"'I overlook your crimes! No one knows better than I why you have dedicated your days to a wicked life and no one could despise you more deeply. You have been unfaithful to me; you have branded yourself with the most infamous deeds; you have become a monster and you are not content with what already you have done to me, you have taken my money and now you wish to deprive me of my jewels. What do you mean to do, Don Vicente?'

114

" 'To take advantage of this supreme moment and punish you as you deserve,' Silva answered in a defiant tone.

"Doña Telesfora arose and made for the door but it was locked. She knew she was trapped. In anguish, she asked, 'What are you planning to do?'

" 'Sit down,' he said.

" 'Don Vicente, Don Vicente!'

" 'You know me well enough and I shall take advantage of this moment to make you pay for your faults, Doña Telesfora.'

" 'Holy heavens, what are you going to do?'

" 'Punish you as I told you.'

" 'Have pity, Don Vicente. Have pity!' she begged as she fell on her knees.

" 'There is no pity.'

" 'What have I done?'

" 'Arise and read.'

"Don Vicente took a letter from his pocket and handed it to her. Doña Telesfora could hardly read; her whole body was trembling and the words became blurs. She felt death so near that she could not control even her hands. Coming close to a lamp, she read:

My dear Don Vicente:

Your wife, Doña Telesfora, is about to turn us into the depths of the law. She has made public all the secrets which she had about our corrupt lives and there is going to be a devil of reckoning for all of us. If you wish to avoid this you better dispose of that woman. If she remains here any longer, it will be too late for the rest of us.

Your friend,

E. A.

115

" 'And why should you credit this letter? There is no truth in it. I have never even thought of doing such a thing. Do you believe that if I had intended to act in that way, I would have come to you here tonight? I came because I love you in spite of your faults and because you are my husband.'

" 'You do not love me, you are a wicked, devilish woman.'

" 'What words to use on a defenseless woman. Do not torment me, for the love of God! Do you intend to kill your wife?'

" 'Not my wife, my dishonor. Read the words in that letter and hide in shame for your deeds.'

" 'I have nothing to hide. I have done nothing for which to be ashamed. If it is a crime to follow you, if it is a crime to prove my love, if this is unforgivable, then kill me but do not use fiction. I can see that you intend to get rid of me so that you can be free to unite yourself to Flor; I am an obstacle to your plans.'

"Everytime Doña Telesfora pronounced Flor's name, Silva's eyes flashed like those of any angry beast. At this moment, he took a dagger from his belt.

"Doña Telesfora seeing herself attacked, felt a cold chill through her body. She could not move but her lips invoked God's help, 'Heavenly Father, have mercy on me, save me, soften his heart!'

"Silva, filled with anger, took his wife by the arm and shook her violently.

"Doña Telesfora, trembling, half dead, her heart beating fast, saw death approaching at the hands of the beast who had once given her his pledge of love.

" 'I read in your eyes what your soul feels,' he said. 'You did not expect to pay for your betrayal in this manner; the surprise is disagreeable!' And the assassin laughed. The laugh sounded in Doña Telesfora's heart as the echo of approaching death.

116

" 'Well, let us finish this. I do not want to be cruel, it is more generous to kill promptly,' and saying this, he pierced her between the breasts with the dagger. A sea of blood spurted and slowly Doña Telesfora fell on the hard floor.

"Silva watched his victim as the last signs of life disappeared. The face of the martyred woman paled, her eyes closed and her lips half opened gave a deep sigh and in a moment she had ceased to exist.

"Silva was satisfied, he had added another black page to his life of crime.

" 'All is ended,' he said. 'If the dead could be grateful for the privilege of dying, this unhappy woman would thank me and forgive me for the favor I have done her. She would sooner or later have betrayed me. Now, I am safe.' And he joined the men in the next room.

" 'What is our program for tonight?' questioned El Patas de Rana, Froglegs.

" 'I don't know,' answered Silva, 'but I have done away with this woman and now I need help to dispose of her body. We must give her decent burial as it is fitting to a group like ours.'

"The bandits entered the room where Doña Telesfora's body lay and El Mellado, after looking at it for a moment said, 'How well our chief handles the dagger.'

" 'Yes,' said another, 'he is an expert in the art. If Captain Esquibel should cross his path!'

" 'I would make him dance a jig,' answered Silva, who had not forgotten that he had turned him in for the theft of Refugio's horses.

"Silva opened a belt which he had tied around his waist, took out some money and handed each man a ten dollar bill, saying, 'prepare to give burial to that unhappy woman.'

117

"He ordered them to wrap her in some blankets and a shawl and then to follow him. He led them to the Campo de Los Cadillos, field of burdocks, which is about a quarter of a league from Los Alamos.

"The Campo de Los Cadillos has a plain runoff, but at a short distance there is a fall of about a thousand yards in width with myriads of narrow arroyos, some with a depth of about twelve feet. Silva, upon arrival, chose the one which he thought would best conceal the body of his wife and there he ordered the body to be lowered. After they pushed the earth from the sides of the arroyo, the body was well covered.

"The burial of his wife finished, Silva ordered his men back to the house. They had gone hardly thirty paces. El Patas de Rana, who was walking beside Silva to his left, upon a given signal, pointed his gun and discharged it at Silva's left temple. Silva fell to the ground like lightning, never to rise again.

"The bandits went through Silva's pockets and belt, and after having taken the money and jewels which he had, they pushed his body without ceremony into an arroyo close by the one in which they had buried his wife. They pushed the sides of the earth upon it and there left him. All was finished; the infamous bandit who had terrorized the citizens of San Miguel and other counties received his well deserved punishment from the hands of the family of devils which he had created and so ably trained.

"After dividing the loot, the criminals dispersed in different directions. El Rana arrived in El Coyote by daybreak; Medrán and Sandoval in Las Vegas, El Moro and El Mellado in their respective homes in Los Alamos. Dionicio Sisneros went to Watrous. The next day, Sisneros borrowed a team and wagon with the pretext of taking his family to Ute Creek, but a few days later he was in Winslow, Arizona."

118

Silva's death did not end the terror from the bandits and it was not until the governor of the territory sent out a proclamation offering pardon to the accomplice or accomplices who would be willing to tell all and a reward of $500 for each of those arrested.

During the second week in April, 1894, the Court started its session and among the trials was that of El Mellado, who had been arrested for robbery. He knew there was no escape and his best chance was to make a complete confession of all the crimes and gain his liberty. He told everything from the beginning of the organization, which was named La Sociedad de Bandidos de Nuevo Mexico, to the current crimes committed at the time of his trial. He testified before the interpreter of the Court, who at the time was Don Rafael Romero from Mora, the district attorney, and my uncle, Don Manuel Cabeza de Baca, who was present.

The confession of the crimes by El Mellado aroused the interest of my uncle Manuel in finding out the details of other events in the work of the bandits. From Medrán he obtained an account of Silva's end and the murder of Doña Telesfora. He proceeded to the place where Medrán told that the victims had been buried. The bodies were found in an arroyo by a field of burdocks near Los Alamos.

The Silva bandits had nicknames or aliases, yet it does not necessarily mean that these names were given to them because of their alliance with crime. The New Mexicans of Spanish extraction are quite fond of giving nicknames to everybody around them. Sometimes they may be pet names, but more often they are given in ridicule.

My first trip to Los Alamos was for the wedding of Uncle Manuel's son, Florencio. It was in 1905 and we were riding in the same carriage as Don Manuel. As we went by the arroyo, he pointed it out to us saying that it was there Silva and Doña Telesfora had been buried. The evil doings of the bandit were always a topic of interest to our family, for it was an era never to be forgotten by the respectable citizens of Las Vegas and surrounding country. As I remember, only those who lived in the perilous days could appreciate peaceful living which came with the turn of the new century. By 1900, the men who had been at the head of the political parties that tolerated corruption had passed on or had lost prestige, yet it seems that honest men were always in the minority in San Miguel County. I grew up in an atmosphere of political chaos to the point that even though I try to be liberal in my political views, my childhood experiences will not allow me to even consider voting a certain political party and I will not vote a turncoat either.

Don Manuel Cabeza de Baca was very influential politically in his early life. In his late years and after writing the Silva story he lost ground. In 1901, he moved his voting rights to Guadalupe County where he spent at least three months during the year and most of his law practice was in that county. He wrote the Silva story in English also, but for some reason or other, he never published it. His daughter, Eloisa Cabeza de Baca de Gallegos, has it in her possession and I have had access to it.

Don Manuel died in 1915, a disillusioned man. The men he helped to climb in politics betrayed him and were responsible for his downfall.

12. Incidents

BILLY THE KID HAS BEEN GLAMORIZED in song and story. In the eyes of respectable persons, he was never a hero. As I remember, he and Vicente Silva were hardly mentioned except as criminals by members of my family. As a matter of fact they were hardly worthy of mentioning at all. I am sure that a great deal of history has been lost due to the hatred our family had for criminals or even politicians who were supposedly respectable but had dual personalities—and there were many of them. This I have learned after leaving the shelter of our ancestral home.

One story about the time of Billy the Kid, I heard from a woman who had been a servant in my grandmother's sister's home. She was our next door neighbor and she was like one of our own. Her grandfather had been a bond slave in my grandmother's home and her whole family had to serve out the bondage. Once they were free, they still worked for the family in some capacity or other.

This woman, I shall call her Remedios, delighted in telling how one day she was washing clothes by the acequia for her mistress. An American rode by and said to her, "Go with me?" "Yes," she said, and off she rode with him. He took her to Fort Sumner and there she lived with him. I do not know if she was married to him, but she had children by him. He was one of Billy the Kid's partners and she was in Fort Sumner at the time that Billy was killed by Sheriff Garrett. She was one of the chief mourners, as she used to tell us. When she started her tale of adventure, grandmother sent us to bed and later would say, "If Remedios had any decency about her, she would not tell the story of her life. I do not want you children to listen to her." She was a marvelous storyteller and full of humor, but our puritanical rearing made it almost impossible to delight in her tales.

Another story of Billy the Kid, I heard from a man whom I shall call Ramón and who worked on the ranch. When Ramón was a small boy, he and his brother used to freight goods to the Indians at Bosque Redondo, now Fort Sumner. One night he was sent to the store to buy candles. Billy the Kid was there and when Ramón finished his purchase, Billy approached him and asked, "Where is the poker game?" "In our camp," he replied. Billy said, "Tell your brother that I will be there to win all his money." He went to the camp and after playing all night, he lost heavily, but took it good naturedly. As he remembered, Billy always had someone outside watching while he was in a game or in some hall, bar or house. Another impressive account which Ramón gave was that Billy found it too dangerous to sleep inside a house. He and his henchmen slept always out in the brush with their guns across their bodies.

GEORGE ECHOLS lived in the Trementina country, not far from Las Vegas. Very few people, if any, knew him intimately. He lived as a recluse, and his neighbors scarcely ever saw him.

In the late summer of 1914, the notorious Carter brothers went to his ranch with the excuse of buying cattle from him. Echols took them out on the range to show them what cattle he had for sale. After the trio rode about a mile from his ranch, one

122

of the Carters pulled a gun on Echols and the other brother hand-cuffed him. They then rode on for fifty miles until they came to Luciano Mesa at the head of Bull Cañon, which is part of the Ceja of the Llano. That part of the country is rough and rugged, and broken trails are few. At that time, only cowboys in search of strays penetrated the Bull Cañon country.

Echols was taken to a lonely half-dugout on the rim of Luciano Mesa overlooking the cañon. At that place the mesa is about a thousand feet high and very steep. One of the Carters tied Echols to the beam which supported the roof of the cabin, with a trace chain padlocked to one of his legs. The other Carter headed for the Echols ranch where he hired three cowboys with shady reputations and rounded up the cattle—Echols' entire herd. The cattle were driven to Montoya, a town not far from where Echols was held prisoner, while one of the Carters watched him.

The other brother shipped the cattle to Kansas City, Missouri, after they were inspected by an inspector with no scruples. Upon the brother's return with plenty of money in his pocket, the two Carters departed for Mexico.

In the meantime, Echols was left alone and he managed to slip the chain off the beam to which it had been tied. The chain was still locked to his ankle, but he was able to make it into Montoya after having been captive for two weeks. On the day he arrived in Montoya, my brother, Luis, happened to be doing our monthly marketing and buying. He heard the story from Echols who had stopped at a ranch house, where he had the chain sawed off.

Two or three days after Echols had come to Montoya, H. L. Thurman, a citizen of the town, received a letter from the Carters in which they enclosed the key to the padlock and instructions as to where they had left George Echols. They enclosed a ten dollar bill to pay Thurman for his trouble.

Echols lived in fear that the Carters would return and finish him off, but they soon got into trouble in Mexico. They crossed into Luna County in New Mexico, where they were arrested and turned over to the San Miguel County Sheriff, Lorenzo Delgado. They were tried and sent to the penitentiary in Santa Fe.

Cattle rustling had been quite a game in the early days and continued for many years. By 1914, the laws had become more strict and the Carter-Echols incident caused quite a sensation. The fencing of the land did away with the stealing of livestock, although once in a while one heard of some rancher losing a few head. After the land was taken up by the homesteaders, the cattle rustlers were more cautious. It was not easy to drive cattle without being seen, as they had to go through someone's pasture or gate and the landowners were forever watching for trespassers.

DON JOSÉ MARÍA BACA was Don Paco Baca's father. He was born in La Cienega in Santa Fe county, but had moved to Chihuahua where Don Paco was born. In his middle age he came back to New Mexico and then lived in Las Colonias. He was a great buffalo hunter and during these expeditions he met a Comanche chief who was known as El Puertas. They became steadfast friends. On one occasion, El Puertas was going to Las Colonias to bring back a horse Don José María had given him. He was also taking an Indian girl as present for the Baca family. She was a captive from an enemy tribe. About a mile from the railroad station of Newkirk and what was then the sheep and cattle ranch of Don Antonio José Gallegos, El Puertas encountered a group of Indians from Bosque Redondo who were on their way to their former hunting grounds on the Llano. The Indians killed and

124

scalped him and took the Indian girl with them, for she was one of their tribe. They hung the scalp to a juniper stump as they traveled east, and many an old-timer used to point out the stump as the one on which El Puertas' scalp hung. Santiago Vigil from El Valle, one of our neighbors, showed the stump to my brother and he pointed it out to me.

Soon after the murder, Don Paco and a group of buffalo hunters, came by on their way to the hunting grounds. They buried the body in an arroyo called Arroyo de las Cuevas.

In the 1920's a grandson-in-law of Don Paco found the skeleton, which had been uncovered by the erosion of the soil on the arroyo banks. Don Paco, who then lived in Puerto de Luna, came to view the skeletal remains and he was sure they were those of El Puertas.

V. WITHIN OUR BOUNDARIES

13. Mustangs

AFTER THE LAND WAS FENCED, a new page was turned in cattle history. Papá became aware that quality rather than quantity would be the salvation of the cattlemen.

The cattle in the days of the unfenced range were descendants of the cattle brought in from Mexico by the Spaniards. In the early sixteenth century, Spanish cattle had been brought into Mexico from the island of Santo Domingo. These were the longhorns, a breed which by necessity had become hardy. They could resist all types of climates and during droughts, if far from watering places, they could go several days without water. If the grass were scarce, they could subsist on hardy desert plants. These cattle were ferocious-looking animals, of great stature, bony and thin flanked. Their long horns, gave them their title as a breed, but in color, they had no particular identification; there were brindle cattle, dun colored ones, white, spotted and black animals. The longhorns being natural rustlers, the cowmen did not have to upset themselves about the welfare of their stock; the cattle managed to survive all sorts of difficulties.

They were not heavy, and, in order to bring good prices, the steers were left on the range to grow to maturity before they were driven to market or sold to the buyers. To derive a com-

126

fortable income, the cattle owners had to run hundreds of animals, but that was not difficult when the range was free and extensive.

I do not know if these longhorn steers were vicious, but they had a wicked look and many a time I climbed the windmill tower when a bunch of them came to water.

The boys derived a great deal of fun from seeing me sitting up on the tower, for I always wished to be considered brave. I lived in the land of storytelling and I wanted to be like the pioneer women who settled the sparsely inhabited sheep and cattle country.

I remember one morning a herd of steers had kept me up in the windmill ladder for almost two hours. I came into the house, meekly trying to avoid the sneers of the boys, but El Cuate took my side.

"It would not be so funny," he said, "if those steers had trampled you and turned you into dust. They cannot be trusted; it is lucky that you had a place to escape to."

Papá joined him in his sympathy as he said to the boys,

"I have been thinking it is time we were improving our cattle. These animals have to be kept in the pasture too many years to be worth anything.

"A great many of the cattlemen have already started breeding their cows to Hereford bulls and the cross is a good one. If our herds are improved, we can diminish their numbers and derive as much or more profit as we did when we did not have to limit the numbers."

Luis replied to Papá's discourse by adding:

"We have to face the fact, also, that our grass will feed only a limited number, so the sooner we improve our stock the better it will be for our land. Our pasture is already overgrazed."

Some of the boys thought it was just a notion Papá and Luis had absorbed from reading, but El Cuate agreed with them. He had worked on ranches where they raised thoroughbred cattle and he gave Papá the names of men who had bulls for sale. It was not long before Spear Bar Ranch boasted of registered bulls.

Each morning, the boys rode out in the pastures to make sure the cows had not jumped the fences. Fences were substantially built with posts cut from junipers on Papá's land. Three or four wires were stretched from post to post; each post was placed fifteen or twenty feet apart with *entremedios* to keep the wire from sagging. Even though the fences were strong, there was danger of the cattle jumping over, as they were not used to being held within one pasture.

In the late summer, Papá went out with the boys to cut hay on the meadows. If we had good rains, the grass would grow tall enough to make hay. It was necessary to feed the cattle in the middle of the winter, at least those who might come out poorly. Cottonseed cake was coming into use, but the hay helped to supplement the ration, and it was easier on Papá's pocketbook.

The land was divided into winter and summer pastures, and in this way grass was available at all times unless there was a drought.

In the days of unfenced range, the cattle watered in the arroyos, springs or water holes. Now, Papá had to drill wells, put up windmills and build tanks to provide water for the stock; there was not an idle moment on the ranch.

We had many horses, and they had been bred from the early Spanish mustangs into different types. But the best cow ponies were those in whose blood was that of the early horses of the plains. A good cow pony must be swift, and the imported horses

128

were heavy and needed training to learn to head off cattle. We had palominos, paints, duns, bays and many others. The boys had their favorite horses and were closer to them than to their best human friends. Each boy on Papá's ranch had from ten to twelve horses as *remuda*. I had my own horses, too, but they were gentle ponies. True to my aristocratic rearing, I had to lead a ladylike life and should not resemble that of our uncouth neighbors whose women were able to do men's work. I always envied any woman who could ride a bronco, but in my society it was not done. How skillfully they saddled a horse! I often watched them catch a pony out in the pasture, just as the men did on our range, but it never was my privilege to have to do it. When I arose each morning, my horse was already saddled and tied to a hitching post waiting for me if I cared to ride.

The horses which were not used as *remuda* or for ranch chores, roamed wild in our pastures. When new horses were needed, they had to be broken. I remember José Gonzáles of statewide fame, who came to our rancho to break horses for Papá. On one occasion, José broke ten horses for us. He kept the ten horses on *persoga,* that is, tied to a pole. The horses were tied with horsehair *reatas* because hemp or rawhide ropes shrank when they got wet. (Often, I helped Papá make hobbles and *reatas* from horsehair by turning the *tarabilla,* a sort of spindle, for him.) Each day José *cabalgaba,* mounted, each of the ten horses, but only one horse went through the tactics of horse breaking.

José Gonzáles went from ranch to ranch breaking horses for the different owners. By 1899, before my time, his fame had become quite widespread. In that year, at Las Vegas, he gave an exhibition of his skill as "bronco buster" at the Rough Riders' Reunion when Colonel Theodore Roosevelt was guest of honor.

Since that day the event has become an annual affair, called the Las Vegas Cowboys' Reunion.

Cattle inside of fences take care of themselves, but there was always work for the owner and his men. Fences had to be kept in repair to prevent the stock from wandering into other pastures; gates had to be kept shut, and we had many gates in all parts of our land; the windmills had to be oiled and repaired constantly. There were arroyos to endanger the cows. These were not a great menace when cattle were fat, but if cattle were poor and they became bogged down, they might perish if the boys did not find them in time. The range had to be ridden daily; the boys watched for missing cattle. One single cow could cause several boys to ride for a week in her search.

It never failed to amaze me to hear the boys discuss the cattle as they came in each evening after the day's ride. They had a name for each cow, or some way to identify her, and there were several hundred. To me, they were all white-faced and dun-colored, but to the boys, each had an individuality. If one single cow was not grazing in its accustomed place, they searched for her until she was found. Often the cow had strayed with another bunch, but if she were not found, the boys reported it at head-quarters and the next day all the men kept on the lookout for the missing animal. With the fencing of the land, there was not much cattle rustling, but the cattle owner took no chances.

HOUSEKEEPING on the rancho fascinated me when I was very young. There was not very much of it. Breakfast was the most important meal and that was a real one consisting of cereal, eggs —lots of them, stacks of hot cakes, piles of bacon, fried potatoes and plenty of coffee. The cooking utensils were all black on the outside. Meals had to be prepared in a hurry for a hungry lot of cowboys and the pots and pans had to be placed next to the wood fire.

On our part of the Llano, there was plenty of firewood, for we lived just over the Ceja from the real Llano land. We had juniper and piñon trees and it was a matter of a few hours to supply the rancho with a week's or month's supply of dry wood.

El Cuate was the ranch cook, but his duties were not con-fined to cooking alone; anyone was cook when he arrived and no food was ready. All the boys could cook. I am sure Papá was a good cook, too, but he had turned this job over to the men who helped with the ranch work.

There were no regular hours for meals. One never knew when the men would cover the vast territory over which the cattle roamed, although, by the time the sun came up, they were well started on their daily roundup. It might be three, four or five o'clock in the afternoon before anyone returned. Beans were a common fare and anyone remaining at the ranch house kept the pot boiling until the others came home. We had beans with plenty of salt pork in them. This was a summer dish, for in the winter, beef was eaten at all meals.

As each boy left his bed in the morning, he rolled it and put it away for the day. Papá and my brother had bedsteads, of course, but their beds were made only when they were changed. Usually after they arose, they pulled the covers over the pillows, and the beds were ready for the next time they were to be used.

The men on the rancho were careful about sweeping the house once a week, whether it needed it or not, as they often remarked. They washed dishes after meals and Papá was a fanatic, as the boys thought, about scalding the dishes. He did not see a need for washing them on all sides, but they must be scalded.

Our mother had died when we were babies and our Spanish grandmother had reared us in the most fastidious manner conceivable. If she had known how well adapted I was to carefree housekeeping existence, she would never have permitted my summer vacationing on the rancho. But as I grew older, my former rearing became evident and I made new rules, which the men resented but accepted meekly.

BRANDING time was the most delightful experience, for then Papá allowed me to ride with him after cattle. I shall never forget my first ride on a real cow pony. I was so proud of having graduated to that degree, and, as we were bringing a bunch of cattle for branding, an animal strayed from the bunch and my horse made a rush for it, as all cow ponies always do. Not prepared for the quick sway, I came down on *tierra firme*. Papá kept the secret for a long time, but when it escaped him, I had to hide myself, until the men had their attention turned to more serious matters.

It took several days to round up the cattle for one day's branding. These were put into the big corral and kept there overnight. The bawling of calves and the bellowing of cattle, from the time they were driven into the enclosure until they were turned out, when the branding was finished, resounded in the air, with only an occasional coyote yelp to change the tone of the noise. On a quiet night, it was wonderful to be lulled to sleep by the bellowing music.

Branding was a social gathering as well as a necessary task. It took many men to perform all the usual jobs of driving the herds, separating them, roping, throwing the animal down, branding, earmarking and castrating. We had neighbors who still had small herds and they came to help. Sometimes the women came along, too, to help with the cooking. I remember times when twenty or thirty persons were gathered at our rancho. It was quite an event, for in the evenings, although the men were tired, there was an exchange of gossip, stories of early "cow punching," killings, cattle rustling and pioneering in the prairies.

UNTIL 1915, there were still a few sheep owners who had their flocks east of us, and who came from Las Vegas to visit their holdings. Our home was a stopping place for the night, and, to me, this was a page from a fairy tale. They were sad people, these men, for their days on the Llano were numbered. Papá and El Cuate would converse about them after they were gone and I knew that one day they would not be coming through.

The priest from Puerto de Luna came occasionally to say Mass in the few chapels of that day, at El Valle, Benavídez,

Newkirk, Cuervo, and at the Pedro Romero Ranch. These were built in a late era to provide a place of worship for families who took up land in the early twentieth century. Sometimes, Papá would take me to one of these places to hear Mass and it was an event never to be forgotten. Families came in carriages, wagons or automobiles, men came on horseback for the festivity. The *patrón,* or owner of the chapel, was host to all visitors. Food was served after the Mass, and the old custom of feeding the men first still prevailed. I always sat by Papá and the women and girls eyed me with curiosity.

My summer vacations seemed so short, and before I realized, I had to go back to school and leave the land that I loved.

The trip of about one hundred miles to Las Vegas, by carriage, took two to three days, depending on the horses and, of course, the weather. We had to prepare for the journey such food as could not be cooked over a campfire. Coffee had to be ground and bread baked for our three meals each day.

The trip was delightful. We were up at dawn in order to take advantage of the hours of coolness, and naturally we had to cover as many miles as possible during the day. Thirty miles in one day was average travel, but fast horses might make forty. Papá loved his horses too well to drive them fast.

The horses had to be watered and rested, so Papá, or whoever was driving the team, always planned the trip so as to stop where there was water. It might have been a water hole in the open spaces or a rancho on the trail. While we ate our noon meal, we rested the horses for at least an hour. The horses, after being watered, were turned into the grass for a snack.

Our stopping place for the night was determined by the availability of water and pasturage for the horses. If rain overtook us, we had to seek shelter in a house. I liked it better when we stopped under the sky for a roof. Sleeping with the stars above was more interesting and cooler, also. How peaceful it was outdoors! The horses were hobbled, so that they might not wander too far, and often a cowbell was tied to the neck of one of the horses. The sound of the bell and the hobbled horses is the sweetest lullaby I have ever heard. A distant, or sometimes near, howling of the coyotes was the only other sound which might break the silence of the great outdoors.

Morning seemed to come too soon, and yet, one could hardly say it was morning, for when Papá called us, the stars were still in the heavens. How cold the mornings are on the Llano, even though the temperature may rise to one hundred degrees in the daytime!

The people along the trail were friendly and hospitable. They welcomed us with open arms, for they seemed hungry for outside intercourse. On the road there were still many large ranchos, since the homesteaders had not invaded that part of the country. Their land was on the Spanish and Mexican land grants. They were far from the railroad centers and those seeking land had not discovered the routes to those hidden spots.

On this road, we encountered chapels which served the ranchos for many miles. In El Chirisco lived Don José Gonzáles, father of the famous *mesteñero,* wild horse hunter, Don Teodoro Gonzáles. At the time that I knew Don José, he was blind, but he ruled his household and *empleados* as a king rules his realm. A room set aside for the purpose of worship on the Gonzáles hacienda, stood as a monument to the faith of the early settlers. Surrounded by the homes of Don José's sons and *empleados,* the Gonzáles hacienda was a village in itself. Don José ran thousands of cattle on his domain. I remember hearing during conversation that in 1906 he had branded one thousand colts. These colts must have been the descendants of the *mesteños,* the wild horses, which had roamed the Llano country in vast hordes over the unfenced land.

I can still recollect when wild burros were hunted and killed for soap making on our rancho and, as a small girl, I often heard the boys tell of horses inhabiting remote canyons close to our land. From them and Papá, I learned the stories of these *mesteños.*

As the buffalo hunters went into the Comanche country, they sighted droves of *mesteños.* They took word back to the settlements and when horses were needed, expeditions were formed to go into the Llano to capture wild horses.

The expeditions usually were made in the spring of the year, since at that time the horses were poor and easy to run down. The men hunting for *mesteños* brought fat, swift horses, making the chase not as difficult as it might seem. With a good horse, the victims soon were overtaken. They were roped with *reatas,* lariats, and once roped, they were easy to get down. They were then hobbled with strong horsehair ropes. There was a special way of hobbling, quite unlike the usual way used for tame horses. The rope was tied from the horse's tail between its hind legs and to one of its front feet above the hoof. This was called *gavilla.* This type of hobbling kept the horses from running away. Sometimes the *mesteño* was tied neck-to-neck with a burro. The sturdy ass was a good match for the wild horse, and rarely, if ever, did a horse get away when guarded in this manner.

Mesteños on the run were a magnificent sight to behold, those who followed the sport related. Every bunch of mares was led by a stallion, and that animal showed its importance as the leader of the herd. He was hard to follow; he was superb as he

136

defended his *manada,* his herd. Once caught, the horses were not as beautiful as they appeared when running. There were all colors of horses, but the dun predominated.

These horses seemed by instinct to know when they were being hunted. The leader of the band seemed at times to have given his *manada* a warning, for so swiftly did they disappear that the hunters were not sure of their prey.

There were some famous *mesteñeros* who could drive a whole herd of wild horses with little trouble. They claimed that once away from their habitat the horses became shy and easy to handle.

No greater *mesteñero* ever lived, perhaps, than Don Teodoro Gonzáles. It is said that he made those around him feel that it was an easy sport. At the first throw of the *reata,* he had his horse, and as swiftly, he was off his horse and down came the *mesteño.* His own horse, of course, was a superior one, but it took great skill.

As the land became fenced, the wild horses were a menace, for one horse out-eats two or three cows, and the cowmen had to conserve grass. Many wild horses were killed, and another Llano sport passed into history.

There were many other ranchos on our way to Las Vegas, but the Gonzáles hacienda stands more vividly in my memory than the others. Perhaps because Don José was such a courteous, hospitable person.

14. "Milo Maizes"

THE RAIN CEASED AFTER THREE DAYS of good drenching and the land took on a new aspect. In a week, the grass seemed to have grown inches and the cattle were happily grazing and putting on slick covers on their bodies. Ours was a happy household!

The ground became dry enough for the boys to resume their daily labors and Papá at breakfast was making plans with El Cuate and the boys for the day's work.

"We shall start fencing on the Pajarito today," he said to the boys. "Cuate, you and Luis will go with me to survey the land, while Pedro and Nereo haul the wire and posts. It will be several days before we will be ready for them, but you can start digging the post holes."

I was delighted, for I would ride out and explore new country. Contrary to Spanish custom, Papá always allowed me to go wherever he or Luis went. The men were always kind and I ruled the rancho like a queen during my summer vacations. There was so much unwritten history of the Llano, and as I rode out in the pastures, ruins of houses and chapels made me wish they could speak so that they might tell of the life of the inhabitants who had dwelt within. But they were silent and I had to

138

create in my mind imaginary characters living in these lonely ranchos. Yet they may not have been lonely; there may have been much gaiety and real living with nothing to disturb their tranquillity.

The country not only held in secret the lives of the Spanish colonists, but of the Indians who thousands of years before had inhabited the land. There were the petroglyphs depicting human figures, animals and other signs. What did they mean? In my mind, I would decipher the figures to give directions towards where the enemy were encamped or where there was a spring of clear water for the nomads—or were they nomads? I would often picture villages of happy primitive people living abundantly from the soil with no destructive civilization to mar their joyful lives. I lived in the past as I roamed the range and studied the petroglyphs. These may have been relatively recent, for in the rocks were deep grooves where the women ground the maize into meal.

My brother and I hunted for arrowheads and other artifacts and these we found in profusion. Luis has a fine collection of arrowheads, scrapers, awls, points, axes and grindstones, and all these were found in our pastures or within a radius of fifty miles.

While the men were fencing, I was free to wander into secluded canyons and caves and to acquaint myself with the wonders of country new to me. Yet those before us certainly had known it well but had left few records for posterity.

We had to fence our lands, for the country was being settled, and where once the boundaries over which our cattle grazed had been the earth's horizon, now we were being pushed in and in, until it became necessary to build fences.

In the pre-Hispanic era, the Llano Indians walked—with the Spaniards came horses and the life of the Indians changed. Then

139

came *Ciboleros* using *carretas* pulled by oxen to go into the Llano for their meat supply, and later wagons with horses began to wind their way over the Llano's rough roads.

The railroad came through Las Vegas in 1879, and the Santa Fe trail, with its caravans of ox wagons, passed into history. The plains Indians were on reservations and life became tame for the New Mexicans who had traveled over the trail. Las Vegas became an important railroad center, but it also continued to be the market for sheep, cattle, wool and hides from the Llano country.

Over the Vega Hill, where Señor Mariano daily played host to travelers, came hundreds of wagons to trade in the Meadow City, yet many of the sheep and cattle from the Llano were driven to Liberal, Kansas, where the Rock Island Railroad had its terminal. From Liberal the stock was shipped to Kansas City, St. Joseph and Chicago.

In 1900 the Rock Island was being built across the Llano country, and by 1901 it had reached Santa Rosa, where it connected with the El Paso and Southwestern to El Paso, Texas.

The land of the Comanches and the *Ciboleros* underwent great changes in the years 1900 and 1901. The Rock Island gave contracts for the building of its lines. Camps dotted the Llano country from Kansas into New Mexico. These camps were a bedlam of foreigners, where many tongues were spoken. There were Italians, Austrians, Greeks, Slavs, Chinese, Negroes, Mexicans, and of course, Americans.

Men were killed by rocks from blasting, and it is rumored that many a man lies buried in the fills of the roadbeds.

On the Pajarito ranch of Don Nicasio Cabeza de Baca, my late uncle, one of these camps was located. There was a commissary in each camp, but there were many articles which were not carried in their stock. My uncle took advantage of the opportunity and set up a store in which he carried clothing and food.

The Italian workers had great confidence in him and when payday came, they turned their money to him. He took it into Las Vegas for deposit in the bank, and a great deal of it he sent to the families of the workers. My aunt, Doña Isabel Stephens, Don Nicasio's wife, tells that when the money started rolling in, she feared a holdup, since there were many bad men among the workers. Until Don Nicasio was ready for the one-hundred-mile trip to Las Vegas, she kept the money in her baby's carriage under the mattress. They did not have a safe and she felt that no one would think of disturbing the baby if someone came to rob them.

There were two really bad characters in the camp, and these were a Filipino and a Mexican. One morning, as Don Nicasio started on his monthly journey to Las Vegas, he saw two men standing on either side of the road, a mile or so from the camp. It was still dark, but he recognized them as the Filipino and the Mexican of bad repute. Don Nicasio always carried a gun by his side, and before the desperados had a chance to point their guns, he had his in his hand. He ordered them to move on. Don Nicasio was not alone in his carriage, a niece was riding with him to Las Vegas. Perhaps the criminals did not recognize in the darkness that the person was a woman, for they quickly disappeared.

Many incidents happened in the year that the camp was located on the de Baca ranch, but considering the many hundreds of laborers and no officers of the law, it was quite peaceful.

A young man from St. Louis, Missouri, who came from a wealthy and influential family, strayed into the camp as a laborer. He was refined and highly educated and why he was there, no one knew. One day, while working, the foreman of the crew became angry at him because he did not work as fast as the other laborers. The foreman used a horsewhip on him. The boy swore that he would have revenge. That night he decided to avenge his wrong, and knowing where the foreman was lodged, he approached the tent. It happened that, for one reason or another, the foreman had changed tents and the boy shot the wrong man, an Italian worker. The boy hid in some caves in the near by hills and there his buddies supplied him with food and water. There was a search for him, but he remained safe in his hiding place until the first flat cars rolled over the tracks. One evening, one of his buddies came to pick up the boy's baggage at the de Baca home, where he always kept it. No one ever heard about the mysterious boy again. Mrs. de Baca says that the boy's luggage was of the most expensive type of its day and often, when the boy came to the house to get clothing, she noticed that his clothes were such as only the wealthy could afford.

The workers lived in tents and the camp manager with his family lived in a dugout which he built for their abode. The Italian workers were very economical and usually saved all of their wages. They lived on bread, rabbits and tea made from snake brush (*gutierreza teunis*). They used milk in their tea for extra nourishment. Ruins of the mud ovens which the Italians built for baking bread can still be seen on the old de Baca homestead.

The land on the Llano is not for the tenderfoot, and an incident which happened at the camp proves it: A young easterner came as office secretary and on the first night of his arrival, a thunderstorm, such as can be experienced only on the Llano, struck the area. Lightning and thunder, followed by a cloud-

142

burst, kept him awake in his tent all night. In the morning, as he was rolling up his bed, two rattlesnakes were coiled under it. He took the next stagecoach for other terrain.

At the time the railroad was in process of construction, the Mesa Redonda (Round Mesa) Brothers, notorious bandits, were making stops at the camps all along the way robbing and pillaging. On one occasion, two of them stopped at the de Baca store, where they bought lunch goods. No one could have picked them out as lawbreakers, for they had pleasing personalities. They wore elegant clothes and their fingers shone with diamonds. They must have been bold to make their appearance in broad daylight where they planned to make a holdup. They were heavily armed. That evening they held up a Mr. Buckley, who had charge of the camp commissary, and got away with more than three thousand dollars. To the de Baca's they were friendly and left them unmolested, although there they could have found more money than in the railroad commissary.

These bandits lived on Mesa Redonda, just over the bluffs of the Staked Plains. The flat top of the mesa is extensive, comprising ten thousand acres or perhaps more. There the bandits kept stolen cattle, horses and other loot. It is very rugged with only one or two accessible places and these the brothers kept carefully guarded. They lived there from 1901 until 1907, when the homesteaders began to populate the country. On top of the mesa, there are several natural lakes and *aguajes,* water holes, which made it very convenient for the robbers to live unmolested.

AFTER the coming of the railroad, many towns sprang up along the way over the Ceja and across the Llano. Tucumcari, today one of New Mexico's larger cities, came into being because of the railroad. Santa Rosa was, because of its location, the logical

143

point for the railroad shops—and they were built there. But, unfortunately, the hard water of the Pecos river at this point was not usable for the desired purpose and Tucumcari profited from Santa Rosa's misfortune.

Santa Rosa and Tucumcari grew into towns and many small towns benefited by the coming of the Nesters, at least for the duration of the influx of the homesteaders. Montoya, named after the Pablo Montoya Grant and situated within its bound-

aries, was an important trading center for some twenty years. The few cattle and sheep owners, the homesteaders and railroad section hands living on the Ceja, traded in Montoya. There was a large general store, several smaller ones, a drug store, two hotels, a three-room public school, a newspaper, a land office, a country doctor, one or two Protestant churches, and the one Roman

Catholic chapel—which still exists and is a *visita* of the Tucumcari parish. Montoya was a busy place while the money of the homesteaders lasted and until the droughts put the stockmen out of business. Today, Montoya is a ghost town and survives only because of U. S. Highway 66 and the few railroad section hands who make up its population.

Cuervo, another railroad station, is the trading center for the ranchers from Garita, Cuervo Creek and others who are running sheep and cattle in the surrounding country.

The people of the vast Conchas country—which lies northeast of Cuervo Creek—formerly traded in Las Vegas. After the coming of the railroad over the Llano they turned to Cuervo and Santa Rosa for the shipping of their wool, sheep and cattle.

The decision of the courts about land grants, the coming of the homesteaders, the railroad over the Llano and the building of highways, caused a transition in the history of the Ceja and the Llano. Amarillo and Tucumcari grew into cities and Las Vegas remained static, contented with one main highway and the crossing of the Santa Fe railroad through its boundaries. Many of its inhabitants little know that once it was the largest trading center in the vast State of New Mexico.

With the coming of the railroad over the Llano, immigration started. Caravans of covered wagons dotted the country over the buffalo and Comanche trails. Another people came to settle where once the New Mexicans of Spanish extraction had lived, where they had found the promised land for their flocks and herds. Gone were the sheep and only a few cattle ranches remained.

PAPÁ was unhappy as he saw the shacks of the newcomers rise on the acres which had been his pastures.

145

Papá was in good humor when we started out one day, but as we reached the place where they were going to start surveying, his mood changed, for just a quarter of a mile from his boundary line, a wooden cabin had gone up overnight and then Papá was infuriated.

Angrily, he alighted from the wagon and turned to El Cuate, saying:

"If those 'Milo Maizes' have put their house on my land, they shall rue the day they came here. They will ruin the land for grazing and they will starve to death; this is not farming land."

"Calm down, Papá," I said. "Wait until you find your boundaries and then get angry. These people have a right to file on the land. You have always owned land, thousands of acres; they are entitled to their half section."

"No one has a right to ruin pasture land and those idiots in Washington, who require that they break eighty acres for farming, are to blame for these poor fools destroying the land. It is a crime for these misguided people to try to make a living in a country that does not have enough rain for growing crops," papá answered.

I felt sorry for the homesteaders. Young as I was, I realized that they could not make the land provide them with even a meager living. I had grown up with a ranch background, where sheep and cattle furnished our livelihood, and I knew the hard times Papá and Grandfather had endured in order to survive. Then, we had control of the land, and only that had saved us from destruction. I knew that, along with the "Nesters," we were due for a transition. They could not exist from farming and we could not increase our herds in the land that was left for grazing. Papá had been resourceful and had acquired all the patented land available, school sections and what he could file for a home-

146

stead, but this was not enough. We had to think of droughts and when they occurred we had no lands toward which the cattle could be moved. On the Llano, unless it is very unusual, droughts are not general; there are always spots where it rains when others are dry. In one's pastures there are rainy and dry spots, and the pioneer sheep and cattlemen knew them.

In 1901, after the coming of the railroad, the Rock Island line promoted colonization into the land it traversed over the Cap Rock. Chartered immigrant cars brought a big colony of Iowa farmers. In the cars came draft horses, farming implements, dairy cows and household furnishings. These people were good farmers, but the Llano country was not farming land. The horses did not become accustomed to the country and neither did the dairy cattle. The Iowans built good substantial homes, but their endurance soon gave out and in order to prove up on the land, they commuted for $1.25 per acre. In three or four years, all but a handful moved to other states or went back to their homeland. Papá liked these Iowans and counted them among his best friends. He bought a great many acres from them upon their departure.

When the Enlarged Homestead Act was passed, families from Texas, Oklahoma, Arkansas and other Southern states began to look towards New Mexico as the land of promise. These families had been sharecroppers or tenant farmers in their own states and to own the land was their most cherished dream. By saving and skimping, they accumulated two or three hundred dollars in cash. With a wagon, a team of horses, chickens, possibly a milk cow and their household goods, they joined other caravans and the march started toward the Utopia of their dreams.

Our rock house may not have been elegant, but it was a

mansion compared to the lowly shacks which the newcomers built. These were merely roofs over their heads and sometimes they did not have even protection from the scant New Mexico rains. There were a few who built substantial houses, because they had brought a little more cash, but they, likewise, soon spent their savings.

They were kindly, simple folks, these homesteaders. Their hospitality was boundless, and Miss Fabiola and Mr. Luis were idolized by young and old. My brother, Luis, and I loved them, but El Cuate and Papá kept aloof, never quite understanding what Luis and I saw in those uncouth people.

A few of the colonists were of the better educated class. Their standards of living were above the average, and Papá did not fail to pick them out as he had the Iowans from the others whom he called "Milo Maizes." This name he gave to those he disliked, because, milo maize was a hardy crop they planted for feed. It was introduced by them into New Mexico.

I do not know why Papá and El Cuate were intolerant towards these humble people, for both Papá and El Cuate were two of the most tenderhearted, sympathetic, understanding and courteous persons I have ever known. May they rest in peace, as El Cuate would say.

Soon after Papá started surveying that morning, an amiable, big husky man dressed in blue denim clothes came toward Papá. He greeted him, saying, "Are you Mr. de Baca of the Spear Bar Ranch?"

Papá was not cordial as he answered,

"Yes, what do you want?"

"I thought you were a white man when I saw you."

Papá, using strong language, replied:

"Of course I am a white man—and an educated one, too."

Papá was tall and very fair skinned. His eyes were the blue of sapphire and his hair was reddish brown. He could not have been mistaken by anyone as not being white, yet these people who came to settle in our midst were ignorant of history. To them, the only white people were those who spoke the English language as their mother tongue.

The man half apologized, not quite grasping his mistake, but I came to his rescue. In Spanish, I spoke to Papá.

"Please, Papá do not hold it against him. He does not know any better; I am sure he meant no disrespect. We have to live among them and we might as well live peacefully."

Papá replied to me, "You can live among them. I intend to fence my land and stay within it."

I knew he could not mean what he said, it was all said in anger. But years after, I knew he meant it, for he never mingled with them—yet he did not forbid us from making friends with our new neighbors.

The man tried to be friendly and addressed Papá again,

"Mr. de Baca, I would like to borrow a milk cow from you. You have so many of them and I can take good care of one. And I would like to haul water from you-all's well in this pasture."

"Do you have children?" papá asked.

"We have five young 'uns, Mr. de Baca," answered the man.

"Come to the ranch house tomorrow and I shall have a cow for you. If you haul water from my place, be sure you close the gates," Papá replied in a resentful voice.

To us he said in Spanish, "I am doing it for his children."

There were many families already hauling water from our wells and many were milking Papá's cows. We did not have dairy cows, but some of the range cows were good milkers and they provided milk for us and the newcomers.

149

Fence after fence went up and soon all our land was enclosed within our own boundaries.

In spite of the hardships, which to the homesteader may not have been such, these people were happy and easy-going. The women worked right along with the men in the fields; they milked the cows and tended the poultry. Their housekeeping was poor, for they had miserable houses with which to contend, but they were excellent cooks, considering the scant variety of food which they had. They knew how to utilize their milk products in many ways and all other food they managed to make

palatable. With all my home economics training, I could not compete with them, perhaps because El Cuate took care of our daily diet.

If today I can fry chicken, make sour milk biscuits and corn-bread, I owe it to the friends of my youth on the Llano.

These people did not build chapels, as my people had done, yet some were very religious. As in any settlement, there were various types of families. There were the churchgoers and those not affiliated with any church; there were those who danced and those who positively considered dancing sinful.

But whether they danced or not, life for all seemed blissful. I never heard them complain about the heat or the drought or hard work. The churchgoers met in the schoolhouse for prayer meetings and Sunday school. This was not only a religious cere-mony, but also a social gathering. The women brought food, and after services the families spread out their victuals and all ate together. The congregation then separated into neighborly groups, exchanged gossip and then went home to get ready for another week of toil.

In the summer, there were "Singings" among the religious groups. Neighbors would gather in some house any day of the week. The young folks played games and sang songs early in the evening; later, young and old joined together and sang hymns. About midnight, refreshments were served and then the guests departed.

The "Singings" reminded me of our *velorios*, when we gather to pray and sing on the eve of some saint or to ask special favors. Ours is more formal and quite solemn, but it is very much a social gathering. At midnight, we serve supper, after much praying and singing of hymns.

The dancing groups met together at the schoolhouse or some

151

house for a night of swing. The dance started as soon as it became dark. The ranches were six to fifteen miles distant and the dancers came by wagon, carriage or horseback. We had to leave home before dark, for although horses have good sense, it was not safe to venture in the dark. We danced until daylight, for we needed to see the road to avoid accidents, or perhaps, we liked to dance so well that a few hours did not suffice. At midnight, the men made coffee by a campfire; the women brought cakes and we certainly had a feast.

On Sundays, the non-church families took turns in going to some home to spend the day. The women always helped with the preparation of the noon meal; the men played cards and sometimes the visits lasted until midnight.

My brother and I divided our time with all groups and although there was animosity among them, Mr. Luis and Miss Fabiola were heartily welcomed whether to a prayer meeting, singing, or dance.

In the summer, we had enjoyable picnics, celebrating the Fourth of July or just for a Sunday outing. Sometimes there were as many as twenty families together.

Although I did not live in the days of the Spanish fiestas on the Llano, I have happy recollections of the days of the homesteaders. My brother and I belonged to a different age from El Cuate and Papá. Both eras were colorful and both contributed much to the history in the land of the buffalo and the Comanche.

Hardly a day went by but some new family arrived, until nearly every inch of ground was taken.

There came droughts and the settlers found it harder and harder to exist. The little money which they brought with them was soon exhausted, and the merchants in the small railroad towns started to give credit to the farmers, with the hope of getting the land in return, and it did not take long for them to acquire it at a low price.

The few cattle and sheep men who were left and who had not been foresighted, had to diminish their herds and they also had to live on credit from the country store. One by one, they also disappeared and Papá would say:

"Someday the land will be washed away, for there is no grass nor shrubbery to protect it. I may not live to see it, but you young folks will realize why I have been so perturbed over this colonization by the Nesters." But he did live to see it, for when the "Dust Bowl" became a menace, he was here to see his predictions become a reality.

The homesteaders were a persistent folk; they plowed and planted and lost their seed, but they stayed on three or four years, or at least until they made final proofs on their claims. A handful remained, but others, although late, realized that their Utopia was a cruel land ready to suck the last trace of hope from them.

One by one they departed, and Papá bought or leased acres and acres of land from the disillusioned colonists and his pastures increased to good proportions, but it was bad land. So much of it had been plowed it would be years before grass would grow. The merchants in the railroad towns became the cattle kings, although some of them had started in the mercantile business with less money than one Nester had brought to see him through. By sagacity they had built up fortunes and the land was theirs.

The homesteaders further east were more fortunate, or perhaps more enduring, for today as one travels towards the Texas border, one sees wheat and other grains swaying with the wind. They have seen some hard times, but such is the lot of those who live from the soil—yet they have taken roots as Papá had on his land.

15. A Country School

MY SCHOOL DAYS WERE OVER and I had come to the rancho to stay. It was a changed place. El Cuate had passed on to a better land and new faces greeted me as I arrived.

Automobiles had come into use, but the roads were in poor condition and only the Model T Ford could make the high centers which were still prevalent—reminders of horse and buggy days. The Ozark Trail traversed our land, but there were no automobile roads to travel over into the neighboring ranches.

It had never occurred to me that schools in rural areas were different from those which I had attended.

I had not been home very long when I began to learn that the children around us had from five to seven months of school and that many of the teachers in the county did not have even an eighth grade education. Education in our family had always been mandatory; that other children did not have the same opportunity as I, did not seem fair to me. When one of the school directors came to solicit me to teach school in our school district, I felt privileged. Papá was not so sure that it was the proper thing for me to do and it took a great deal of pleading to gain his consent. In giving it, he stressed that if I signed a contract I had to

154

live up to it and, whether I liked it or not, I had to stay the full seven months. He was certain that after I found out what the environment held for me I would repent, but I was determined to keep my word.

The schoolhouse was six miles from our ranch, but six miles was a great distance on horseback, and I could not ride back and forth each day. It meant that I had to find a boarding place.

One family lived close to the school—they were simple folk, but very gracious. They arranged to give me room, board and laundry for twelve dollars. My salary was seventy dollars a month, paid in warrants which could be cashed at ten percent discount at the bank in Santa Rosa. Since Papá was able to pay my bills, I kept the warrants for several years—until the county had enough funds to pay.

The school was governed by three school directors and one of these resented my appointment as the teacher for his school. What my qualifications might have been did not concern him, since he had a *compadre* who had taught the school, and schools were given to teachers not for merit, but because they might be relatives or belong to the right political party. I did not understand all this and little did I care. The joy of teaching and helping those around us, although I had hardly realized what it meant except in ideal surroundings, was my ambition for the moment.

I had a huge room with a bed in one corner, a small table, an improvised washstand, possibly two chairs and a niche with a beautiful *bulto* of San Miguel. The floor was of hard-packed mud with not a rug to relieve the bleakness of it. I might have longed for my room at home—my cozy bedroom which I had decorated in the latest style—yet if I wished for it, I did not admit it even to myself. I was going home every Friday. Why it did not occur to

155

me to take furnishings from home, I do not know, but perhaps the reason was that, even as a youngster, I could not bear to hurt anyone, particularly those who were poorer than I.

The one-room school stood in a lonely spot among the junipers and piñons with Mesa Rica as a background. It was built of rock with four narrow windows, two on each side. The room was so devoid of furniture that a weaker heart might have been disillusioned, but I remembered my promise and papá's warning.

There was a desk for the teacher and a chair which was held together with bailing wire. The desks for the pupils were all the same size and each held three to four children who had to share it together.

The children came to school from ranches—two, three, five and six miles distant; a few drove in buggies or rode horseback, but the majority walked.

Our first chore was to clean the schoolhouse, and the children were as eager as I to tackle the job. We scrubbed the pine floor, washed the desks, cleaned windows and swept the yard. While sweeping the yard, we had the fright of our lives—close to the door was coiled a six-foot rattlesnake. When I heard the rattles, I flew into the schoolhouse, but soon the children had it under control—with a blow from the hoe the snake was decapitated. The weeds had grown up to the door after the summer rains, yet carefully, the larger boys cleared the growth making sure that no more snakes were there to scare the teacher. Some of the boys must have been nearer to my age, but they were as obedient as the younger ones.

It was a mixed school. There were the children of the home-steaders, the children of parents of Spanish extraction and children with Indian blood but of Spanish tongue.

When the room was in order, I started to seat the children

156

according to grades. Luckily, only six grades were represented, as in those days few of the pupils stayed to finish the eight grades.

This was a new experience, but by the end of the week I was as settled in my work as if I had been teaching a lifetime. The children were very docile and, in general, very adaptive.

Notwithstanding the distances the children had to travel to come to school, they were there early to help the teacher bring water, sweep and dust the school room. In the winter there were fires to be built in the wood stove.

We opened the morning and afternoon sessions by singing and the children loved it. The Spanish children knew folk songs and the Anglos, cowboy ballads and hillbilly songs. As a reward for good lessons, we sang these, but I also taught them songs which are sung in school nowadays. *The Star-Spangled Banner* resounded on the Mesa Rica each school morning. We had a small flag, but we had not yet heard of the Pledge to the Flag.

There were few diversions at these scattered ranches. Therefore, school programs were well patronized; I soon learned this from the children and we began to plan for a Thanksgiving function. Our school had started in October so that the children would have finished helping with the harvest.

At first I had fifteen children enrolled, but when the word spread that I was the teacher in the Benavídez district, pupils from other districts started to come. I had a Normal School education and that was more than very few, if any, had in the whole county. And as I said before, the majority of the country school teachers had not even completed grammar school. Much was expected of me, but I was having fun.

I soon became acquainted with the children, and by the second week of school I was receiving invitations from different ones to go and spend the night with them. I certainly appreciated that, although it meant walking several miles and getting up before daylight in order to get to school in time to sweep, dust, and haul water before nine o'clock. It was adventure and I was getting plenty of it.

During some weeks I did not sleep in my boarding place more than one night. But when I did, I enjoyed it; I could then have a sponge bath. I read, corrected papers, or sewed by lamplight, and the family with whom I boarded dropped in to talk to me. Every individual is different and one can learn something from each one. I am sure that I underwent one of the best educations anyone could receive. I learned the customs, food habits, religions, languages, and folkways of different national groups. They were all simple, wholesome people living from the soil. They certainly were a hardy lot, for otherwise they could not have survived the cruelty of the wind, the droughts and the poverty which surrounded most of them. They asked my advice on many subjects but I never felt capable of giving it to them. My education was from books; theirs came the hard way. It was superior to mine.

I taught reading, spelling, history, grammar, arithmetic, physiology, penmanship and geography.

In my Normal School education, I had been trained to teach reading by the phonetic method, but I had nothing like a phonetic chart. From my practice teaching notes, I improvised some charts and had a difficult time with the few beginners as their parents knew that the alphabet method was the only way to learn reading. They may have been right, but I taught phonetics and the children were able to read in a few months.

The classes had to be combined whenever possible, as there were too many grades for one teacher to handle. Spelling and reading were combined in all the grades, all the primary pupils in one and the intermediate in another class. The sixth graders had all their classes separate from the others.

American history was an important subject from the fifth grade up but the textbooks stressed American colonial history, and since that is the way in which I had learned it, I made a good teacher. One sentence or perhaps a paragraph told about the Indians and the Spaniards in the Southwest. The children learned about the Delawares, the Iroquois and the Mohawks, but learned little about the Comanches, Apaches, Navajos or the Pueblo Indians—and the teacher knew not much more, except by absorption through family conversations and fireside story-telling in her home.

The geography lessons were strict in the fifth and sixth grades; the pupils had to learn the name of every state and territory and their capitals. Each one knew the industries and products of the states as well as all the large rivers, lakes, oceans and principal mountains of their country. European and Asiatic geography were not neglected. The pupils could name every country and its capital. They knew where the Dead, the Red and the Mediterranean seas were and what races populated each country. I am sure that those sixth graders knew more about Mexico, Central and South America than the average high school graduate knows today.

I know they knew more grammar than many college entrants do now. I say this from actual teaching experience in later years.

The pupils learned about germs from their physiology lessons and every sixth grader had to learn the names of all the bones in the body from the cranium to the phalanges.

Reading was interesting in all the grades. The textbooks had stories with morals in them and many were quite dramatic. The children cried over many of the stories. As a reward for good lessons, I allowed the children to dramatize "Little Red Riding Hood," "The Three Bears," and others from their readers.

Poetry must have been one of my favorite interests as it is today, for I made every child learn one poem each week, from the first grade to the sixth. These were later used for school programs.

We had no books for supplementary reading, as they do today, but we managed quite a library by buying the "Progressive School Classics" at a penny apiece. The children brought their pennies, I ordered the books, and we contrived quite a collection. I have today in my library copies of many of these booklets and tears come to my eyes as I remember my first country school. In a "Child's Garden of Verses" are marked the names of the children who had to learn a certain poem in it. We learned to sing many of Robert Louis Stevenson's verses.

In our collection we had the stories of the great men in history, and as I look back, the teacher and the pupils had a well-rounded general education.

For a blackboard, we used pieces of black oilcloth which had become so badly cracked that I wonder how writing on it was possible.

The pupils had to be very careful with their paper and pencils. It was almost a day's journey to Montoya and most of them had to count their pennies. Each day before school was dismissed, I collected all the tablets and pencils and each morning a pupil was assigned to pass them out. We had no automatic pencil sharpeners, but the larger boys performed the chore of sharpening them with their pocket knives.

For drinking water, we had a bucket which a monitor was responsible for keeping filled. As well as I can remember, there was a common drinking cup for all, including the teacher. Physiology failed there, but the parents would have resented it if I had used my own cup.

A can of water was kept on top of the stove which heated the room. This was used to scrub the hands of the pupils who had failed to do so at home. In general, all the children were meticulously clean but occasionally one escaped his mother's notice upon leaving home.

I remember one child biting me once when I was scrubbing his hands. They were chapped badly and it must have hurt him. His brothers told it at home and next day the father came to apologize and to ask me to punish him before all the pupils. It was not necessary, and I did not believe in corporal punishment. There was not a bad child in the school. Discipline is obtained with love and I had plenty of it for each and every pupil.

There was no privy for the school and when I told Papá about it, he went to one of the school directors and told him to have one constructed. The director told Papá that it was not necessary—there were plenty of junipers around the schoolhouse.

The weekly spelling match was something toward which the children looked forward on Friday mornings. The contest was conducted between boys and girls from the fourth grade up. How they studied for it!

Morning and afternoon recesses were great events. We played baseball, singing games, Hide and Go-Seek, Run Sheep Run, the Farmer in the Dell, London Bridge Is Falling Down, and many others which I have forgotten. Every pupil took part in all the games. We had several baseball teams, as I remember.

We had bi-lingual readers for the primary grades. These were the adopted texts of that day. In this way, the English-speaking children learned Spanish and the Spanish-speaking learned English.

161

The best method for teaching reading was for the pupils to read aloud. This was done in order to teach correct pronunciation of the languages. The Spanish-speaking pupils in all the grades had had very poor training in pronunciation, and the beginners knew not one word of English. It is amazing how well both groups learned each other's language in just seven months of school.

The *th* in a word was difficult for the Spanish-speaking children to pronounce. Hours were spent with them pronouncing *this, that, with, those, them* and similar combinations.

I taught addition and subtraction by the number table combination method which was similar to the multiplication tables that all the children had to memorize beginning in the fourth grade.

Grammar was very important, with sentence analysis, parsing and conjugation of verbs. How I remember trying to break the children of the homesteaders from using a singular verb with a plural noun, and to say "Guy and I," instead of "me and Guy!" How very important it was to me that they speak correctly!

I had to improvise the busy work for the children. Those who have followed teaching as a profession well know that children must be kept busy all the time or trouble will brew for the teacher. I brought magazines from home. *The Ladies' Home Journal, The Mentor,* and others with pictures. The third graders made geography books from the pictures and from them learned about people in other lands.

When the small children became tired, I let them go outdoors to play until time for their lessons. Outdoors, they gathered pretty rocks to represent cattle and horses, and we had a big rock corral built to put them in. We also built a rock ranch house which kept them busy building and tearing down. The house had barns and corrals and even a mud oven. We had plenty of shrubs to select from for the landscaping and the children were never idle.

This was an election year, and I mention it because the school was the center of it. My uncle was running for governor of the State. I had lived in an atmosphere of political influence, yet I never had witnessed an election nor thought much about it, except as something which excited the populace.

Some member of my family had always been a candidate for office, but politics belonged to the men. This was the second election since statehood, and my uncle was the incumbent vice-governor. I believe I was his favorite niece, at least he trusted me with some of his most important business affairs. I kept books for him, signed checks and measured type in his newspaper establishment when I was fourteen years old and only in high school. Later I was his private secretary on Saturdays and after school hours. He was a slave to the cause of the poor people and no one, perhaps, knew it as I did. In those days, being a member of the political party to which my uncle belonged in San Miguel County was indeed martyrdom. But we had many great men who were martyrs to the cause and my uncle was one. It took courage year after year, to run or support that party, yet when New Mexico became a state, my uncle was one of the men selected for one of the high offices and he was victorious.

Elections were held in the schoolhouses in the country places, and the eve of election was celebrated by a big dance by both major parties. Our school was chosen for the *baile,* and the voting was to be held in the neighboring school of the precinct.

Just before the dance broke up, a party of politicians arrived

163

to announce that the voting place had been changed to our schoolhouse and Papá was furious. The ranches were far apart and only those attending the dance would know of the change and many votes would be lost. It had been a trick of the *politicos* of the opposing party, for they had already notified their people.

There was one automobile within a radius of twenty miles, but luckily the owner, Don Vidal Ortega, was on our side. There were all those people who lived on top of the mesa and the church people who did not dance. The roads were so bad that fewer families could be reached by automobile than by horse, but we had many horses.

It must have been three o'clock in the morning when we planned our itinerary. Papá was the *patrón* and we were all ready to obey his orders. My horse was saddled and I was sent to take word to those on the mesa five or six miles distant. It was not a pleasant journey at that time of day and less so when I had not had experience in opening gates. On my way back, I was told to stop at the Ortega ranch to pick up a beef which they would have ready on my return from the *ranchos* assigned to me. With no sleep that night, only the excitement of my mission could have kept me awake.

By eight o'clock, I was back at the Benavidez ranch and ready to help with the cooking, for we had to feed all who came to vote. Although women did not have the ballot, whole families drove to the voting places. It was an important event in their lives, and one of the few social gatherings in which everyone would concur.

Whiskey flowed freely and the men were feeling quite happy. It took several drinks for some of them to decide which way they would vote. The voting place was not far from us, but a hill made it impossible to see just what was happening. However, we were kept informed of events, as the *politicos* had a private room for conferences in the house.

At noon we fed every man, woman and child who had gathered at the voting place: Republicans, Democrats, Anglos, Hispanos and others.

In my scrapbook, I keep a ballot, which thirty years ago I marked for a souvenir, and it shows that one hundred twenty-three ballots were cast, and of those, my uncle received seventy-six. The precinct was definitely on the opposite side from the ticket on which my uncle was running, but the homesteaders stood by us one hundred percent. I know that some of our *empleados* and the young man to whom I was betrothed did not vote for my uncle.

In the evening, while the election judges were counting votes, the atmosphere around the polls became hotter than a one hundred degree sun. Men with plenty of drink became quarrelsome. It is unbelievable that men who in daily living seemed so calm and peaceful could become as fierce as beasts over an election. But it was so, as I remember that election in 1916. Certainly these men could have had nothing against a man who had devoted his life to the cause of the underprivileged, but such is the way of the populace.

OUR first school program was successful. The mothers gave generously of their time to help. We improvised a stage in the front part of the room by curtaining it off with sheets which the children brought from their homes. Local musicians gladly furnished music for us. Some of the boys played the harmonica and that everyone enjoyed.

I believe my brother took more interest in the school than I did. He would tell me what to do on all occasions, for he knew

the country better than I. For our programs, he was master of ceremonies, and a good one.

After Thanksgiving we started to practice for the Christmas exercises. That, of course, was to be a greater event than Thanksgiving.

On Christmas eve, men on horseback, families in wagons and carriages came and soon the school room was filled to capacity. Lanterns, hung from the ceiling, furnished the stage lights. I wonder, today, how I managed in the small space left for the performance, but everything went on smoothly. In one corner we had a dressing room covered with sheets to hide the actors. Sheets also served as the stage curtain.

How I had the courage to put on a two-act Christmas pantomime is something beyond comprehension, but I had city ideas, and the limitations of a country school did not trouble me.

166

My brother was Santa Claus and he had a bag with candy, nuts and a big orange for every pupil and child who came to the entertainment. No child was left at home, although it meant a long ride home after midnight. It was customary to make the program as long as possible so that the audience would be repaid for their trip.

Papá financed the Christmas treat, for surely I had no money. It would have been cheaper for Papá to have paid my salary and have kept me at home. In those days there were no funds for materials, books or equipment. The teacher either bought them out of her own pocket or did without. Having been trained in a teachers' Normal School, I had high ideals, and Papá's pocketbook was the victim.

The County School Superintendent came once to visit our school. I learned from him that we were using books that were out-of-date or as they said in those days—"not the adopted texts." The children were learning from them and I did not bother to change. The children in general could not have afforded it.

We had pictures of Woodrow Wilson on the wall and the superintendent was upset until he discovered that Abraham Lincoln's picture hung in a prominent place.

But there were Fridays and I went home. Sometimes Papá came in the carriage to fetch me, or if I had brought my horse I would ride home alone. I loved those lonely rides. I would live over the days of buffalo hunting and all the history El Cuate had described so beautifully. I would picture rodeos encamped on spots which I thought might have been ideal.

Soon I was home and my dreams were forgotten. Reality faced me with so many things that had to be done since I was taking my housekeeping duties seriously. The house had to be cleaned, cream had to be churned and there was baking to do.

167

I had to catch up with my reading between darning and patching, but when Sunday afternoon came, the house was in order and I was ready to go back to my teaching.

The children brought their lunch to school and every mother remembered the teacher. There was always an extra sandwich, a cookie, a piece of cake or perhaps only a biscuit with fried salt pork for me. I managed to eat all that food and I did not put on a pound. My weight remained amazingly at one hundred pounds.

Mass was an important event and on that day there was no school. The majority of the children were non-Catholic, but the directors still followed the rule which prevailed before the day of the homesteader.

The chapel had been built and furnished by the Benavídez family and was dedicated to Our Lady of Guadalupe. The Benavídez family had one room especially built for the priest, who always stayed for the night. He came from Puerto de Luna—a good fifty miles. No one ever went into the priest's room, which was the best furnished room in the house. I got my first glimpse of it when the priest came. Besides the host, I was the only one asked to sit at the table for meals when the priest was served.

Not only did I teach the three R's, but I taught the girls sewing and needlecraft, and the boys drawing and outdoor sports.

On a Friday afternoon, on the day devoted to needlecraft, one of the girls sat on a crochet hook and it stuck in her thigh. I was panicky for we were many miles from a doctor and no means of conveyance except a wagon and team of burros which some of the children drove to school.

There was no privacy in the schoolroom and a snowstorm raged outdoors. I managed to hide the girl from the boys by having the girls make a close circle around her. I worked on the crochet hook but it seemed to go in deeper. As I walked out of the circle to get hot water from the stove to clean the blood, the boys were all eyes and wondering what was happening. One of the boys came up to me with an opened pocket knife and said,

"Let me cut her flesh, the hook can only be removed that way."

I almost fainted at the thought, but the boy was serious. I had often watched the boys pick out thorns and yucca points from their hands and feet with pocketknives and to them it was natural.

There was no need for a surgical operation, for by the time I went back to the girl, the hook had worked out and I regained my composure. I would have dismissed school for the day, yet I did not dare for one could not see ten feet ahead. The snow had been falling since noon and now it was sure to continue through the night. Would the parents worry if the children did not go home, or if I sent them on and they lost their way, would I be guilty if any of them perished in the storm? I almost wished I had not compromised myself to schoolteaching, but wishing did not relieve me of the responsibility. Fortunately, we had plenty of wood to last several days. I took a vote from the pupils and it was unanimous that we stay in the schoolhouse for the night.

We had no lamps or candles but the light from the wood stove served us for the night. Our wraps served as beds and covers. I tried to stay awake in order to keep up the fire but I was not alone; the older boys took it as seriously as I did and the fire did not die down. The stove roared all night.

By morning the storm had subsided and the world around was covered by a foot of snow. We were a dismal and hungry bunch. The boys were used to hardships, and as soon as there was enough daylight, they cleared a path to my boarding place.

169

The family there were prepared for our call and soon we had food and water. Snow on the Ceja and Llano does not last long if the sun makes its appearance at all. Soon men on horseback from different directions came to our rescue with food and clothing. They knew we would be safe and I was thankful that they had placed that much confidence in me. Everyday I became closer to the parents and to the children.

The school directors asked me to close for Holy Week. I had not planned to go home and here I had a whole week to spend as I pleased. On Monday evening I went with some of the children who lived five miles east from the school, planning to come back to my room next morning. On my return I found the house deserted and every door locked. I walked to the next rancho, three miles distant, but there I found all doors latched. I was so tired I did not know what to do but I had to keep on traveling. April days are hot on the Ceja and on the path which I followed there was not even a tree to provide shade or shelter. After walking three more miles, I found folks at home and there I stopped but I was already too homesick to wish to stay. I borrowed a horse and rode on to our rancho.

We had only one more week of school after Easter and it was with deep regret that I bade goodbye to the children. As I look back to my first year of teaching, I know I have never been happier and I have never been among people who were more hospitable, genuine and wholesome than those who lived on the Ceja.

16. The Drought of 1918

THE LAND AROUND US WAS BEING ABANDONED. The homesteaders, one by one, had given up trying to make a living from farming and had departed to other regions. The ground which had been plowed became hills of sand and nothing grew but tumbleweeds.

The wind seemed to blow harder than ever, but this may have been because there was nothing to hold the dirt from blowing.

I knew Papá had been right when he said that the plowing of the land would destroy it for pasturage.

The spring of 1918 had come and gone and no rain. There was no grass and the cattle were in poor condition. The two previous years had been dry and, although Papá had fed his stock and rented pastures for them, they had come out poorly.

With the war the cost of living had risen, and flour and sugar were rationed. We had to buy cornmeal to stretch our wheat flour allowance. It was a hard year for the Ceja in every way.

When it is dry, the sun seems to burn up what little vegetation there is. The cactus and mesquite had always grown in abundance, but now only the cactus survived. Papá and the boys were up at daybreak cutting it and burning off the prickles before feeding it to the cattle.

The men never complained about the work or the heat, but when they came in at noon for a snack, burnt brown by the sun, they were exhausted. My brother would say, "This is God's cursed country and we shall perish expecting to live from the land."

Papá would answer, "We shall pull through somehow. We can always start again when the rains come and the grass takes root. I have lived through many droughts. Cattle have died but I have built up my herd again and again."

The drought spread from New Mexico into Texas, Oklahoma and Kansas, but in the northeastern part of New Mexico on the Ute Creek country, Luis was received by Don Nestor Cabeza de Baca, who, then, owned two townships. There was grass there and Don Nestor offered pasturage for our herd, small compared to his two-thousand head of cattle.

We had to round up the cattle and it took several days to bring them all together for the train ride. Papá ordered the cars for shipping them and they had to be ready on the day the railroad officials said the cars could be picked up.

Papá had already reduced his ranch help, so I had to help with the roundup. It was another experience in my life, as before I had only ridden the range for pleasure or as an adventure. Now it was real work.

It took every hand on the place to drive the cattle, but the hard work began when the animals had to be loaded on the railroad cars. It was a new event for the cows and calves and they rebelled. All day the men had been driving them through the chutes and into the cars. It was very hard labor and when the sun sank behind the horizon they were still loading cattle. Some of the cows almost had to be carried into the cars. These animals refused to move as they reached the chute leading into the box car and it took two or three men to push them through.

After the last cow was safe in its overnight shelter, there were

172

the horses to load in the car provided for them. There were several opinions as to how the horses should travel, whether with saddles on or off. I believe the saddles were put on and taken off at least four times before everyone was satisfied. The horses rode with saddles on. The cattle had to be driven fifty-five miles after they reached Logan, the railroad station.

When the train pulled out and five of our boys were riding the caboose, I broke down and cried. I do not know why, but I felt sorry for the cattle riding so close together in those cars. I knew they would be back, but parting to me has always been hard. Papá was standing beside me and tears rolled down his cheeks when he saw me weeping. We did not speak, but we each knew what was in our hearts. One is never lonely on a ranch while cattle roam in the pastures, but it can become a very forlorn place when one does not see them grazing as one rides the range. I knew what Papá was thinking.

The cows that were too weak to make the trip were left behind and those had to be fed every day. It kept Papá and one other man busy burning cactus prickles and putting out cake for even that small bunch. The other boys would not be back for several weeks.

Our cash must have been very low, but we were concerned only in saving our cattle. We all had to work together to save every penny possible. My sisters, Guadalupe and Virginia, were home on vacation from boarding school and the three of us did work we had never dreamed we could do. But we had to help papá and it was enjoyable. We fussed a great deal as to who had to do what, but we got the job done. Getting up early in the morning was possibly the hardest task for us, but washing, ironing, baking, cheese- and butter-making, and all the other housekeeping along with them, took a great deal of energy, yet they

173

were good lessons in homemaking for us. It was hard on Virginia's beautiful piano hands. She was the family musician. I was the ugly duckling, so it did not matter what housework did to my hands.

Papá was forever watching the sky for signs of rain but there were none in evidence. The few summer showers that came seemed to make the earth drier and hotter. It was a long summer.

The cattle were coming home in the fall and Papá decided to drive them back instead of shipping them by rail. It may have been because Papá had to save money that he made this decision.

My brother had stayed with the cattle and now Papá and the boys who were working for him started on the 150-mile journey to bring back the herd. It took them ten days to drive the cattle back. When they reached the Canadian River, about three miles from the present site of Conchas Dam, the river was up and they could not cross. They had to wait three days before they could venture the swollen stream. On the third day, they took a chance and I have always enjoyed my brother's description of the hundreds of cattle swimming across the red waters, driven by our boys and Papá.

Papá shipped most of the cattle to Kansas City to market that fall, as he knew that not many could survive the winter, and it was well that he did, for in December the snows came. The snow fell and fell until two feet covered the ground. The snow stood on the ground ninety days. There were no cattle left and very few horses lived through the severe winter. And Papá had to start again.

Many cattle and sheep men went out of business in 1918 and few were ever again able to build up their herds. The land began to fall into the hands of men who had made money with the war just passed.

174

When New Mexico became a state, millions of acres became available for sale as state land, but it was a political graft and only those belonging to the right political party were privileged to buy or rent. Papá was on the wrong side, and although he was approached by the political leaders in power to change his party affiliations in order to secure state land, he did not care to do so, and so he lost a chance for becoming a big cattle king with thousands of acres at five cents per acre rental.

Papá had acquired considerable acreage from the homesteaders, but the land had undergone too much erosion and it would be many years before all the plowed and overgrazed land would go back to grass.

With the drought of 1918, even the mesquite had died and the cactus had been depleted by using it for feed. Papá would have to reduce his herd unless he could acquire better land. Underground water was abundant on our pastures and men who had purchased or acquired large tracts of land and had no water, were forever interested if Papá would care to sell.

And Papá did sell; but he had taken deep roots on the Ceja, roots deeper than the piñon and the juniper on his land. He had endured hardships and had stayed on when others had given up in despair. It was not easy for him to become accustomed to another terrain.

He had his children, but they never could be as close to him as the hills, the grass, the yucca and mesquite and the peace enjoyed from the land. He loved solitude and the noise of the cities was not in accord with his life.

Before Papá had finished closing the deal with his buyer, he was buying other land, but small compared to what he had controlled. This was not strange land, for before the coming of the Nesters, it had been part of his grazing acres on the Monte de

175

Pajarito. He would not be far from the hills which had surrounded his former pastures. The same arroyo that had crossed his land, traversed the country into which he was moving. It was as if he had moved over inside another one of his fences. Yet, this must have been hard on Papá, for I remember when we built a new home a mile from the old ranch, he lingered in the old homestead until the last piece of furniture had been removed.

Although our ancestors were adventurers who left their mother country in quest of new lands, yet those of us descended from them are of a stable nature. It takes more than droughts and other hardships to move us. The loss of our lands has been the only cause for abandoning our pastures and farming land, and that has been because we were unprepared to defend our rights when outsiders pushed in.

When General Kearny talked to the citizens of Las Vegas on August 15, 1846, he promised protection for the New Mexicans and their property and the United States in agreement with Mexico. He also promised that the Spanish and Mexican land grants would be respected. But New Mexico, isolated for so many centuries, did not have enough lawyers to plead the cause for its people. The owners of the grants and other lands were unable to pay for the surveying and gradually most of the land became public domain. Unaccustomed to technicalities, the native New Mexicans later lost even their homesteads because of ignorance of the homestead laws, but all this belongs to a subject too vast to discuss in this history of the Llano.

The rains and snows after 1918 did not bring back the grass —there had been too much overgrazing and plowing for Nature to compete with the scant moisture. Papá built up his herd according to the capacity of his land, but droughts came again in 1933. There was no rain from the fall of 1932 until the third of

May, 1935 and the drought was not broken until that winter, when a foot of snow covered the Ceja and the Llano.

The land, between the years 1932 and 1935, became a dust bowl. The droughts, erosion of the land, the unprotected soil and overgrazing of pastures had no power over the winds. The winds blew and the land became desolate and abandoned. Gradually the grass and other vegetation disappeared and the stock began to perish. There was not a day of respite from the wind. The houses were no protection against it. In the mornings upon rising from bed, one's body was imprinted on the sheets which were covered with sand. One no longer breathed pure air, and continuous coughing indicated that one's lungs were permeated with the fine sand. One forgot how it felt to touch a smooth surface or a clean dish; how food without grit tasted, and how clear water may have appeared. The whole world around us was a thick cloud of dust. The sun was invisible and one would scarcely venture into the outdoors for fear of breathing the foul grit.

The winds blew all day and they blew all night, until every plant which had survived was covered by hills of sand.

Papá kept on feeding his cattle, but the day came when his purse became empty and he could no longer buy feed. He became disillusioned and as quickly lost the strength to fight.

The government started buying the cattle and killing off those which were too poor to move. Papá's cattle were in good condition, but he did not know how long they could survive, so along with other cattlemen he had to sell. He could not take it and he became ill of an illness from which he never recovered. For the cows that were killed, he was paid twelve dollars per head; for those that were in good shape he received eighteen and the calves brought six dollars.

177

Papá was past sixty and he knew it would be many years before the land would come back; he knew he could not start again.

The land which he loved had sucked the last bit of strength which so long had kept him enduring failures and sometimes successes but never of one tenor. Life so cruel and at times so sweet is a continuous struggle for existence—yet one so uncertain of what is beyond fights and fights for survival. One has not lived who has not experienced reverses. Papá had a full life.

He is gone, but the land which he loved is there. It has come back. The grass is growing again and those living on his land are wiser. They are following practices of soil and water conservation which were not available to Papá. But each generation must profit by the trials and errors of those before them; otherwise everything would perish.

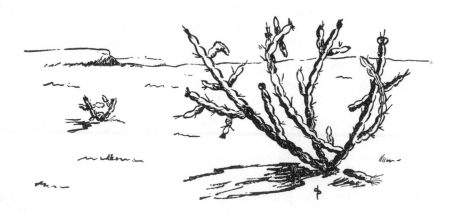

GLOSSARY

Agregado. Assistant, helper.

Baile. A ball or dance.

Bastonero. One in charge of selecting couples during a dance; the director of a ball.

Bulto. A religious statue.

Caballerango. A man in charge of horses during a rodeo.

Caporal. An overseer on a sheep or cattle ranch.

Carrero. Wagon driver.

Ceja. The Cap Rock country.

Cibolero. Buffalo hunter.

Cíbolo. Buffalo.

Comanchero. A man engaged in trade, often illegal, with Comanche Indians.

Corrida. A "run" or "try" on horseback.

Corridos. Folk verses or songs recounting local events.

Cuarto. A quarter of the day; a shift or watch.

Despensa. Storeroom for food.

Empleado. Employee, servant.

Gallo. A rooster.

Gavilla. A method of hobbling a horse; see page 136.

Hacendado. The owner of a ranch or an estate.

Llano or Llano Estacado. The Staked Plains of New Mexico and Texas.

Los Gorras Blancas. An organization so named because its members wore white masks or hoods.

Manada. A herd of horses.

Mayordomo. The manager of a ranch.

Mesteñero. A mustang hunter.

Mesteño. Mustang, wild horse.

Milo maize. *Sesuto maile,* a sorghum grown as grain and forage for stock.

Morada. A Penitente chapel.

Panocha. Sprouted wheat pudding.

Parroquia. Parish church.

Partidas. Flocks of sheep. Each *partida* usually consisted of one thousand head.

Partido. A head of stock taken on shares.

Partidarios. Ranchers who took stock on a share basis.

Patrón. A landowner, employer, or "boss."

Penitentes. A religious group; see page 55.

Politico. Politician.

Reata. Rope, lariat.

Remuda. A string of horses.

Rico. A member of the wealthy class.

Rodeo. A cattle roundup.

Santeros. Makers of religious art.

Santos. Statues and paintings representing the saints.

Tasajo. Dried meat, jerky.

Tejano. Texan.

Vaquero. Cowboy, horseman.

Visita. A rural church without a resident priest.

180

INDEX

183

184

P

Pablo Montoya Grant, 69, 144
Paez, Narciso, 19, 34, 35, 37
Palomas Mesa, 2, 3, 70
Palo Duro Canyon, 1, 41, 49, 67
El Partido de la Unión, 90-92
El Partido del Pueblo, 89
El Patas de Mico, 106
El Patas de Rana, 117, 118
Patrón, Juan, 79
Peña Blanca, 76, 80, 81
Penitentes, 55-56, 72
People's Party, 89
Plaza Larga, N. M., 25, 37, 50, 61, 66, 67, 71, 72
Perea, Don José Leandro, 73
El Puertas, 124-25
Puerto de Luna, N. M., 30, 51, 54, 71, 79, 125, 133, 168

Q

Quay, N. M., 62
Quintana, Juan José, 46
Quintana, Juan María, 33, 36

R

Railroads, 54, 55, 75, 96, 140-45, 147, 173
Red River Chronicle, The, 69
Regis College, 82
Republican Party, 91, 165
La Revista Católica, 82, 83
Revuelto, N. M., 20, 34, 37, 72, 79
Rito Blanco, Tex., 71
Romero, Casimiro, 70
Romero, Eugenio, 69
Romero, Hilario, 48, 110
Romero, Miguel, 81
Romero, Don Pedro, 74
Romero, Pedro, 108-09
Romero, Rafael, 119
Romero, Román, 69
Romero, Trinidad, 69-70
Romeroville, N. M., 70, 103
El Romo, 105
Roosevelt, Col. Theodore, 129
Rossi, Father Alfonso, 83

S

St. Michael's College, 96
Saiz, Carpio, 105
Saladito, N. M., 37, 67, 72
Salcedo, Manuel, vii, 17, 18, 19, 21, 22, 28, 34, 38
Salcedo, Rosa, 34, 38
Sandoval, Agapito, 70
Sandoval, Gabriel, 98, 99, 100, 101, 102, 103, 113
San Hilario, N. M., 30, 31, 35, 36, 38, 68, 70, 71, 74
San Jon, N. M., 67
San Lorenzo, N. M., 19, 30, 32, 35, 36, 68, 69, 70, 74, 79
San Miguel, N. M., 54, 76
San Miguel del Vado, N. M., 77, 80
Santa Fe, N. M., 52, 61, 69, 78, 81, 84, 96, 110, 124
Santa Rosa, N. M., 76, 79, 140, 143-44, 145, 155
Sena, José, 83
Sherman, Gen. William, 70
Silva, Emma, 98-101, 103, 111-13